Great Plains Publications
420 – 70 Arthur Street
Winnipeg, MB R3B 1G7
www.greatplains.mb.ca

Great Plains Publications gratefully acknowledges the financial support provided for its publishing program by the Government of Canada through the Book Publishing Industry Development Program (BPIDP); the Canada Council for the Arts; as well as the Manitoba Department of Culture, Heritage and Tourism; and the Manitoba Arts Council.

Design & Typography by Relish Design Studio Inc.

Printed in Canada by Friesens

Library and Archives Canada Cataloguing in Publication

Gourluck, Russ
    Picturing Manitoba : legacies of the Winnipeg tribune / Russ Gourluck.

Includes index.
Includes 200 photographs from the Winnipeg tribune archives.
ISBN 978-1-894283-76-2

    1. Manitoba--History--Pictorial works. 2. Manitoba--History--Miscellanea.
3. Winnipeg tribune--History. 4. Journalists--Manitoba--Winnipeg--Interviews.
5. Newspaper employees--Manitoba--Winnipeg--Interviews. I. Title.
FC3361.G68 2008   971.27   C2008-902490-7

PICTURING MANITOBA

LEGACIES OF

RUSS GOURLUCK

GREAT PLAINS
PUBLICATIONS

In memory of Gordon Aikman and
Frank Chalmers, Photographers

Photo courtesy Jeff De Booy

Contents

Introduction

by Val Werier

The day *The Winnipeg Tribune* folded on August 27, 1980 remains vivid in my mind. A call was made to stop the presses and all staff was summoned to meet in the newsroom on the fifth floor. This was most extraordinary and precipitous and I was scared that the news we were to hear would not be good. It was shattering. There had been no inkling of this impending disaster. It was kept secret save for the publisher and a couple of executives.

And now we were witnessing the spectacle of the president of the Southam chain hopping on to the horseshoe rim of the news desk so he could be seen and heard by the crowd of employees ranging from the pressroom in the basement to the composing room on the sixth floor. The news spread like wildfire. People streamed into *The Tribune* building – among them my son Michael – to ascertain whether indeed *The Tribune* was no more. Around the province, the shock was profound. Families for successive generations were adherents of *The Tribune*. Staff members were household names. The newspaper was an important voice in the life of the community.

As the first book on *The Tribune*, this edition is welcome indeed. As the title indicates, this was not to be a penetrating study but an affectionate look at a venerable institution. Russ Gourluck succeeds in this vein. His book is a celebration of what *The Tribune* meant to its readers. It is largely a tribute to *Tribune* photographers and is lavishly illustrated with hundreds of photos, an intriguing picture of Manitoba.

I look back at my forty years with *The Tribune* and think how fortunate it is I had chosen journalism as a career. I was immersed in many facets of city life and met people I interviewed decades ago who are still friends today.

As a columnist I was my own boss, choosing topics without interference from the editors, and felt extremely proud when my columns influenced city and provincial governments to take action. I see the mature trees facing the Convention Centre. I persuaded the provincial government to plant a border of trees on its sterile parking lot. Newspapers can initiate good changes in a city.

The pace of life was much slower in the 1940s, a time when the telegram was still used to transmit copy, and type was formed from hot lead by monster linotype machines. This relaxed era nourished strange performances.

Tony Allan honed his golf skills on the second floor of *The Tribune* Building. An errant ball scooted into the open door of the boardroom where a meeting was underway. Tony apologized, gravely picked up his ball and continued his game.

Unlike the restrictions today, readers freely made their way right into the newsroom. They came in carrying giant tomatoes, squash and pumpkins, proud of their efforts and worthy of notice. After being presented with a giant egg, the harried city editor promptly threw the egg out of the open window, landing on a passerby. Furious, the man ran into the building to find the perpetrator. He was directed to the office of the U.S. Consulate, then a tenant in the building.

Windows were open at night in hot weather because there was no air conditioning. One night in flew an owl. Erith Smith, night editor, acted promptly. He secured the owl in a big wire basket used for wastepaper. After work the next morning, he boarded a streetcar with the owl in the basket and headed for Assiniboine Park. There he released the owl.

I have good memories about *The Tribune* and one relates to a dinner with former colleagues at my cottage five years ago. It was a warm affair with wine and reminiscences and fresh fish netted that day in Lake Winnipeg. Frank Chalmers, in his quiet and unobtrusive manner, wandered about, taking a number of photos I assumed for his own collection. Several days later he appeared at my door in Winnipeg with a wonderful surprise.

It was a photo montage, framed in glass, titled "A Day at the Beach." Here is the intimacy with the lake, the gathering of friends, the character of the cottage, the beaming host, the close-up of a plate of pickerel, salad and parsley, all artfully arranged. It hangs in my dining room.

The Tribune, in constant competition with the *Free Press*, gave Winnipeg a reputation of a newspaper town. It attracted writers from across Canada, Britain and the U.S. A lively paper, it generated a number of fine writers and photographers. The irony is that it was gaining circulation in its closing years. Still losing money, the Southams stated that the huge cost of a new plant to forge ahead could not be justified.

It was resolved in a deal with Thomson Newspapers Ltd., which owned the *Free Press*, that in return for closure of *The Tribune*, Thomson closed its *Ottawa Journal*, a losing rival to the *Ottawa Citizen* owned by Southam.

The robust *Tribune* building at Donald and Smith was demolished in 1983 and disgracefully turned into a parking lot because of a lack of vision and understanding of our heritage.

It should have been renovated for residential use, essential to the health of downtown Winnipeg. The location was admirable and blessed by "ecclesiastical" birds – the hundreds of sparrows who streamed in at eventide from various parts of the city to roost overnight in winter on the trees of the nearby Holy Trinity Church. Their spectacular odyssey has never been fully explained.

The spirit of downtown was diminished with the demise of *The Winnipeg Tribune* and the later departure from the heart of the city of the *Free Press*. But the legacy of *The Tribune* will endure, stored in the University of Manitoba and other archives for future generations. They will reveal much of their times and of the journalists and photographers who recorded the Manitoba scene. In their print and images they will show that *The Tribune* was indeed an instrument of vitality and history.

Preface
by Russ Gourluck

Writing this book has, in a sense, been an act of atonement for me. In the late 1970s I subscribed to both of Winnipeg's daily newspapers. My subscription to *The Tribune* was on a prepaid basis, meaning that I periodically received an invoice from the 'Trib' and mailed a cheque. At some point, the invoices stopped coming, but the daily paper didn't. Although the idea of phoning the circulation office to report the situation was somewhere in my mind for several months, it never surfaced into action and I continued to read *Tribunes* for which I hadn't paid.

I clearly remember my immediate reaction on the morning of August 27, 1980 when I heard that *The Tribune* had folded. I hadn't paid my bill, the newspaper was bankrupt, and it was my fault.

The exaggerated guilt I felt for the demise of the Trib was short-lived, but for almost three decades I've lived with the notion that maybe, just maybe, if I and others like me had done our part, *The Tribune* would have lived on.

So putting together this book has not only brought the satisfactions that come with meeting fascinating people, paying tribute to a Manitoba institution, and telling stories that deserve to be told, it has also hopefully helped to repay a long-standing debt.

The main purpose of *Picturing Manitoba* is to showcase the work of the photographers of *The Winnipeg Tribune*. They were people who excelled at their craft and didn't always receive the recognition they deserved. Much of the book is devoted to displaying photographs that were taken for the immediate purpose of illustrating news stories but have, with the passage of time, become enduring records of many aspects of life in Manitoba. They now, in clear and vivid black and white, tell their own stories.

For that reason, I've chosen to keep captions to a minimum, often simply stating the "who," the "where," and the "when." Some photos are accompanied by the wording and date of the cutlines that appeared when they were originally published in *The Tribune*. Others provide some insight from the point of view of the photographers who took them. If this minimalist approach, somewhat in contrast to the amount of detail in my first two books, stimulates the curiosity of readers and motivates them to do a bit of their own research (or at least to draw on the accumulated knowledge of someone older than themselves), then the merit of understatement will have been demonstrated.

Where the names of photographers are available, they appear by the photos. Unfortunately, many of the prints in The *Tribune* Collection don't have the names or have handwritten notations that I wasn't able to decipher. Readers who can solve some of these mysteries by providing photographers' names where none now appear are asked to contact me so we can make changes if, as I optimistically hope, the book goes to additional printings.

I want to thank Gregg Burner, Buzz Currie, Ed Dearden, Jeff De Booy, Vic Grant, Gerry Hart, Dona Harvey, Gerry Haslam, Al Hutchinson, Jan Kamienski, Jack Matheson, John and Betty Robertson, Frances Russell, Jim Shilliday, Jon Thordarson, Peter Warren, and Val Werier for sharing their memories of the Trib. Although not all of the information they provided could be accommodated in the book, their recorded interviews have, with their consent, been donated to the University of Manitoba's Archives & Special Collections to become part of The *Tribune* Collection.

I offer special appreciation to Val Werier for graciously agreeing to write the foreword; to Gregg Shilliday and Catharina de Bakker of Great Plains Publications for their ongoing support and assistance; to Katie Chalmers-Brooks for sharing memories of her father and Gordon Aikman; to Dr. Shelley Sweeney, Lewis St. George Stubbs, and Brett Lougheed of the U of M's Archives & Special Collections for all of their help and encouragement; and to Glenn Marquez and Miko for their patience and proofreading.

The Winnipeg Tribune was an important part of the lives of Manitobans for ninety years. I hope in some small way this volume does justice to the newspaper itself and, more importantly, to the men and women who devoted their working lives to honing their crafts and making it the outstanding publication that it was.

I welcome comments, criticisms, and corrections from readers and can be contacted by email at russgourluck@shaw.ca or by regular mail in care of Great Plains Publications, 420-70 Arthur Street, Winnipeg MB R3B 1G7.

Sources

□ □ □ □ □

Almost all of the photographs in this book were kindly provided by the Department of Archives & Special Collections of the University of Manitoba Libraries and are part of the *Winnipeg Tribune* Collection. These images are © University of Manitoba and reproduced with permission.

There are three main components in *The Tribune* Collection: the small personality files, the large personality files, and the news files.

Small personality files: These are filed in the collection and identified in this book by their names. (Example: Photo of Ed Dearden, page 40)

Large personality files (boxes 1 to 19): These have accession numbers preceded by PC-18. Abbreviated versions of the accession numbers of these photos appear beside them in this book. (Example: Photo of Lillian Gibbons, page 42. The full accession number PC-18-10186-1 is shortened to 10186-1)

News files (boxes 20 to 75): These have accession numbers beginning with PC-18-A81-12 followed by the number of the box, the file, and the photo. Abbreviated versions appear beside these photos in this book. (Example: Photo of *Tribune* editorial staff in 1896 on page 16. The full accession number PC-18-A81-12-66-5660-36 is shortened to 66-5660-36.)

Photos obtained from other sources are credited as "Photo courtesy" followed by the name of the donor.

The publisher welcomes clarifications and corrections from rights holders and will endeavour to rectify errors in subsequent printings.

Ninety Great Years

1

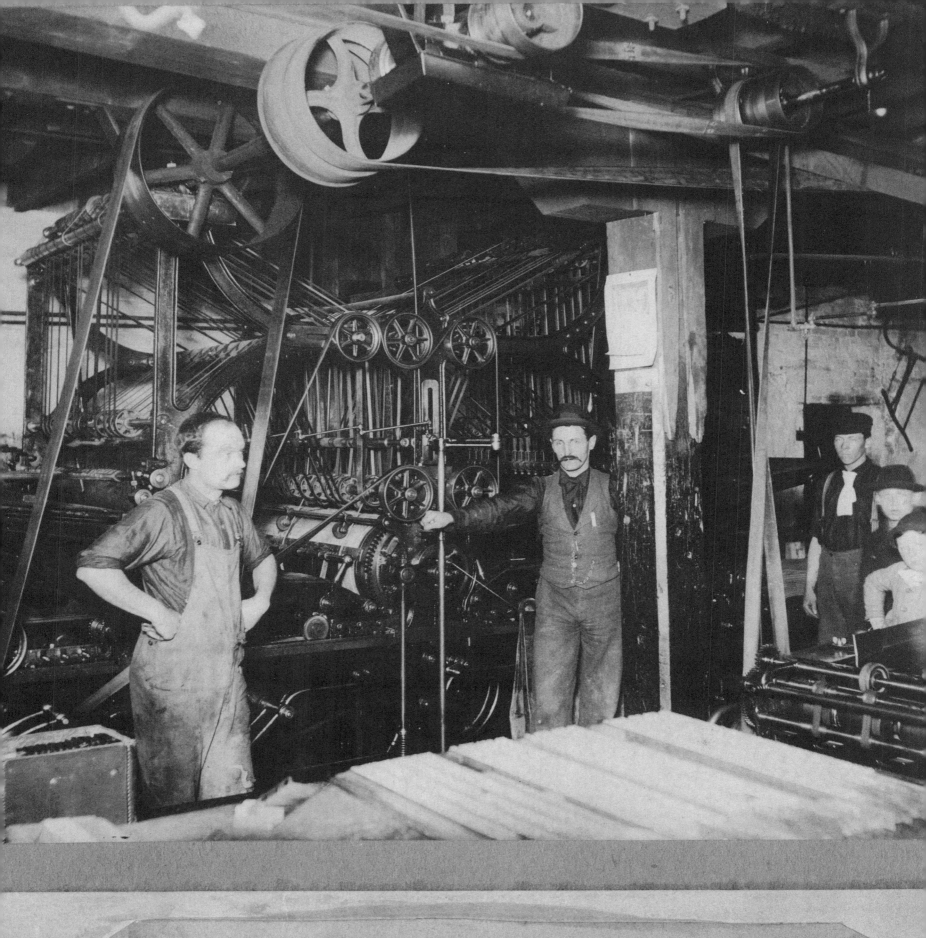

WINNIPEG TRIBUNE PRESS ROOM, APRIL, 1896.

If Bob Richardson and Duncan McIntyre had been prudent businessmen, it's likely they wouldn't have begun to publish *The Winnipeg Tribune*. Fortunately for generations of Manitobans, they were newspapermen with dreams, and the practical realities of business didn't stand in their way.

A Dream in a Newspaper Graveyard

Rising from the Ashes of the Sun

Winnipeg in 1890 was not a good place to begin publishing a newspaper. In the preceding thirty years, approximately twenty papers had appeared and subsequently collapsed. In fact, only one remained – the *Manitoba Free Press*, founded in 1872.

This remarkable rate of casualties was caused by a number of factors, including the young city's boom-and-bust economy, dried-out cash flows, and even the destruction of presses by an angry mob during an especially heated election. The proliferation of papers also meant that there was considerable competition – particularly from the formidable *Free Press*. It's not surprising that John Wesley Dafoe, the *Free Press's* legendary editor from 1901 to 1944, is said to have raised a glass in a toast proclaiming Winnipeg "the graveyard of newspapers."

Among those casualties was the *Winnipeg Sun*, which shut down in December, 1899, just one of sixteen newspapers swallowed up by the *Free Press*. This left its 30-year-old city editor, Robert Lorne Richardson, without a job, and with little affection for the *Free Press*. Richardson, despite his youth, was an experienced newspaperman, having worked for the *Toronto Globe* before moving west, and he saw an opportunity

The Tribune's editorial staff in 1896. At the left desk with his foot on a chair: co-founder Robert L. Richardson; seated at left desk: editor John J. Moncrieff, who was with The Tribune from its inception until his retirement in 1937; shown at the desk on the right: David Scott (standing left) and James Lawler (seated right)

to challenge the monopoly of the *Free Press*. He and a childhood friend Duncan Lloyd McIntyre – they'd grown up on neighbouring farms in eastern Ontario – came up with $7,000 and purchased the premises and plant of the *Sun* at 191 Bannatyne Avenue, just east of Main Street.

One of the reasons the *Free Press* hadn't taken steps to block a rival from buying what was left of the *Sun* was the fact that the old presses appeared not to pose any threat. Richardson and McIntyre had acquired a dilapidated double Wharfdale flatbed press, capable of producing a maximum of 2,500 newspapers an hour on one side only.

Making *The Tribune* Distinctive

The first issue of *The Tribune* came out on January 28, 1890 with an initial run of 2,500 copies that were quickly snapped up on the streets. The city of Winnipeg, population 24,000, once again had a choice in newspapers – as long as Richardson (who was initially both the publisher and the editor) was able to come up with the weekly payroll of three hundred dollars.

By the turn of the century, the *Winnipeg Telegram* had made Winnipeg a three-newspaper city and *The Tribune* had changed its appearance and its offerings. The pages had expanded to seven columns, and single-column headlines had grown to two or even three columns. Recognizing the importance of appealing to women readers, the paper inaugurated a women's page in 1900, with the syndicated "Molly Mayburn's Weekly Page" providing tips on fashions and housekeeping.

The *Telegram*, which first appeared in 1898, was unabashedly Tory in its editorial stance. The *Free Press* was clearly Liberal. This left the position of independence unclaimed, and fortunately that stance matched the personality of the fiercely-unfettered Richardson. But Richardson was quick to clarify in an early editorial that independence didn't mean neutrality. He committed his fledgling newspaper to "vigorously advocate all measures which it conceives to be in the

ROBERT RICHARDSON
AN INDEPENDENT THINKER

It's not surprising that *The Tribune* under the leadership of Robert Richardson adopted an editorial position of independence from political parties. Richardson's own political career, which began in 1896, demonstrates that he wasn't the kind of person who could abide by party rules. Richardson won the federal riding of Lisgar for the Laurier Liberals in 1896, but by 1900 was expelled from the Liberal caucus in Ottawa for openly disagreeing with Liberal railway and tariff policies. In the 1900 election, Richardson ran as an independent candidate, again in Lisgar, and was elected. After that election was invalidated, he ran unsuccessfully as an independent four more times before being elected in Springfield in 1917.

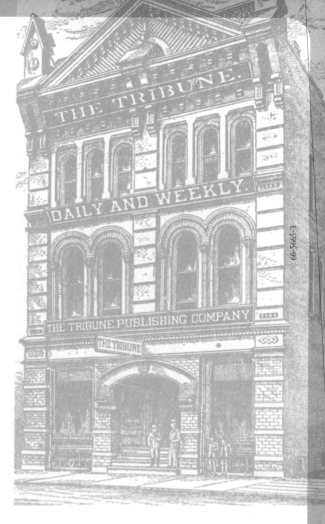

The first home of *The Winnipeg Tribune*, from 1890 until 1901, was formerly occupied by the *Winnipeg Sun*.

interests of the province and to oppose all measures which it conceives to be antagonistic to those interests." Although in later years *The Tribune* would come to be perceived as Winnipeg's "Conservative newspaper" in counterpoint to the *Free Press* as the "Liberal newspaper," the spirit of independence espoused by Richardson would remain with the *Tribune* throughout its lifetime.

Another hallmark of *The Winnipeg Tribune* through all of its years was its focus on local news – one of its first editorials called for improved garbage collection in the city. The local emphasis, however, began as much from necessity as it did from design. When the *Sun* shut down, its access to the Associated Press news service – distributed by the Canadian Pacific Railway over its telegraph lines – was acquired by the *Free Press*, giving that newspaper a monopoly on wire service news in the city. This left *The Tribune* with little choice. To attract readers and to fill its pages, it had to print local news. There were, of course, some stories on the national and international level, but these were belatedly and somewhat illicitly obtained by having contacts in other cities mail clippings from their local newspapers. This piracy was periodically discovered and thwarted by the powerful CPR.

READING THE BLOTS

The Tribune's first news editor, John Moncrieff, a loyal staffer from 1890 until 1937, was in the habit of writing his editorials using pen and ink on newsprint. The resulting blotting and splotching made his handwriting readable to only one man in the pressroom, and when that employee was ill, there was panic in the newsroom.

The Tribune's second home was a former theatre on McDermot Avenue's "Newspaper Row."

PIEING THE TYPE

One unfortunate day in 1893, a *Tribune* pressman was the victim of the worst mishap that could befall a printer – "pieing" (spilling) the type. He slipped and fell while carrying the front page form to the press, and the most important page of that day's edition was scattered across the pressroom floor. With no time to reassemble the leaden letters, staffers scrambled to find completed stories to fill the vacant space. The front page of that day's *Tribune* included no significant news, three chapters of a novel by Etta W. Pierce, and an apologetic notice explaining that the latest news was on the floor.

New Premises, New Presses

By 1901, Winnipeg's population had grown to 42,000, and it would triple in the next decade. *The Tribune* had done more than simply survive for over ten years; it had put itself into a position to move to better premises and to purchase a better press. The newspaper's new location was the former Grand Theatre on the north side of McDermot between Main and Albert – right next door to its rival, The *Free Press*. With the *Winnipeg Telegram* located just across McDermot, the corner came to be known as "Newspaper Row."

In preparation for the move, Richardson had the theatre seats and stage removed. Stereotyping equipment and a Hoe rotary press capable of printing 20,000 papers an hour were installed, giving *The Tribune* the ability to turn out an eight-page newspaper and to incorporate illustrations, graphics, and photographs.

Graham and Smith

On November 15, 1912, Robert Richardson proudly announced that he had "shot the works" with the purchase of a piece of property on the northeast corner of Smith and Graham. A handsome new six-storey building designed by prolific Winnipeg architect John Danley Atchison arose on the site, featuring an elaborate terra cotta facade adorned with 14 gargoyles along the top and a series of 14 heads between the first and

(Left) *The Tribune* Building decorated for the 1939 Royal Visit; (Right) *The Tribune* Building in 1958

(Left) Linotype machine operator Howie Stone (ca 1970); (Right) Getting ready to print (ca 1970)

second floors. When the building opened in January of 1914, a brand new press was proudly displayed behind glass panels — a Hoe sextuple capable of producing 24,000 24-page papers in one hour.

By then, the 'Trib' (as Manitobans had affectionately come to call it), had access to the Western Associated Press, formed in part by a rare coalition of the three Winnipeg dailies. This strange alliance of rivals was necessitated by the heavy-handed 1907 decision of CP Telegraphs to double its rates for the distribution of Associated Press offerings, along with virtually eliminating Canadian content. In 1917, WAP joined with the Eastern Press Association to become Canadian Press. The acquisition of an international wire service enabled *The Tribune* to provide its readers with timely news from the European war front.

Although many of its reporters were absent in uniform during the war, *The Tribune* managed to cover the local beat, especially when fascinating stories like the scandal surrounding the construction of the Legislative Building came along. And once the war has ended, the Winnipeg General Strike rocked the city.

THE BOTTLES ON THE ROOF

Some Tribbers recall that the roof of the addition on the north side of The *Tribune* building was a convenient place to dispose of empty liquor bottles during the winter months. They were simply tossed out of office windows to land, often without breaking, on the soft rooftop snow, and were soon hidden by another snowfall. One spring, after the thaw revealed a formidable accumulation of bottles, an unnamed publisher read the riot act about drinking in the office.

The *Tribune* night desk staff on August 14, 1945, when the war with Japan ended;
(Inset) Putting together a page (1950)

The news desk in 1950. The news editor sat at the horse-shoe-shaped desk to oversee the work of the rim editors on the other side.

REMOVING THE GARGOYLES

The fourteen grotesquely charming terra cotta gargoyles that glared down on the intersection of Smith and Graham from the top of the *Tribune* building were sometimes said to depict prominent 1912 Winnipeggers, but a more likely explanation is that they represented various workers in the newspaper business. Publisher Bill Wheatley was convinced that the gargoyles were designed by Royal Doulton of England.

The 300-pound gargoyles, along with the faces at the second-floor level, were removed in 1969 when the terra cotta façade of the building – columns, scrolls and all – was stripped off to be replaced by pre-cast concrete. This change in the stately appearance of the exterior was precipitated by a consultants' report warning that the five-inch-thick cladding could break loose from its steel moorings and injure hapless pedestrians below. The heads and gargoyles were snapped up by collectors.

The gargoyles on *The Tribune* Building depicted various aspects of newspaper work.

The sale of *The Tribune* to Southam Co Ltd. extended the horizons of the newspaper, enabling it to move in new and exciting directions and to compete with its sole rival.

Southam Takes Over

New Ownership, a Two-Newspaper City

One of the most significant developments in the lifetime of *The Winnipeg Tribune* took place in 1920 when Robert Richardson, who was in failing health, sold the business to family-owned Southam Co. Ltd. for $50,000 cash and $190,000 in preferred stock in The *Tribune* Publishing Company. Richardson didn't live to enjoy many of the proceeds of the sale; he died in November, 1921.

At the time they acquired *The Tribune*, the Southams already had newspaper interests in Hamilton, Montreal, Ottawa, and Toronto. *The Tribune* was to remain a Southam newspaper for the remainder of its years.

Shortly after its sale to Southam, *The Tribune* took over the 27-year-old *Winnipeg Telegram*, leaving the *Free Press* as its only competitor. This acquisition meant, in a sense, that *The Tribune* inherited the pro-Conservative Party editorial position of the *Telegram*. M. E. Nichols, who had been editor of the *Telegram* from 1905 to 1914, became the publisher of *The Tribune* in 1920, and held the position until 1936. The arrival of Nichols also brought *The Tribune* some of the *Telegram's* most capable staff members.

The Southam takeover had a number of benefits for *The Tribune*. Southam almost immediately invested $100,000 in a new press. The newspaper now had access to the reports of Southam correspondents

LONG LANCE, THE CHARMING IMPOSTER

One of the most interesting characters to staff *The Tribune* in the early 1900s was "Chief Buffalo Child Long Lance." Born Sylvester Clark Long in North Carolina in 1890, he claimed that his father was a Blackfoot Chief. He was a charming and handsome man who had his autobiography published, starred in a motion picture, and, although born in the United States, fought in the Canadian Forces in World War One. "Long Lance" was considered a good reporter, and achieved some prominence by writing articles that advocated Native rights. It was eventually determined that Clark's racial heritage was actually African-American.

in other Canadian cities and abroad. At the same time, *The Tribune* expanded its own wire services. These developments placed *The Tribune* in a better position to appeal to Manitoba readers and to compete with the *Free Press*.

Serving the Community

As a daily newspaper with an emphasis on local news coverage, *The Tribune* undertook a number of community initiatives.

During the 1920s, *The Tribune* established the Empty Stocking Fund to help needy families at Christmas time. It became Winnipeg's largest Christmas effort until it was replaced by the Christmas Cheer Board.

During the Great Depression, Community Song Nights were held in city parks over a three-year period. At the beginning of the first season, 10,000 song sheets were printed and expected to last the entire summer; they didn't last the first night. Some of the community sing-songs attracted as many as 60,000 people.

The Friendship League, another Depression-era initiative of *The Tribune*, assisted families on relief. Citizens who were experiencing hard times realized they were still better off than those who were jobless. Thousands of nearly destitute families were "adopted" by others who were at least a little less unfortunate.

During the legendary 1950 flood, souvenir *Tribune* photo editions went through seven printings, for a reported total of 228,706 copies. Proceeds were donated to flood relief.

A newspaper-reading class in 1962

Outdoing the *Free Press*

The Tribune's ongoing competition with the *Free Press* (or "the other newspaper," as each discreetly called the other in print) was waged in several arenas. Circulation and advertising had important financial implications for both papers, but for the people who produced the contents of the newspaper, having better stories and better photos was the main goal. And the ultimate thrill for Tribbers came in scooping the *Free Press*.

On one occasion, *Tribune* reporters unexpectedly learned of the dramatic capture of some bank robbers, but only after the front page of the morning edition had already been laid out with a story stating that the hunt for the robbers was still in progress. Knowing that the *Free Press* always picked up one of the first bundles of *The Tribune* to come off the press, they arranged for fifty copies to be printed with the obsolete front page. *The Tribune* then quickly replated their front page to carry the updated story. The *Free Press*, fooled by the bait, ran a story about a manhunt-in-progress, and only *Tribune* readers were aware that the capture had already taken place.

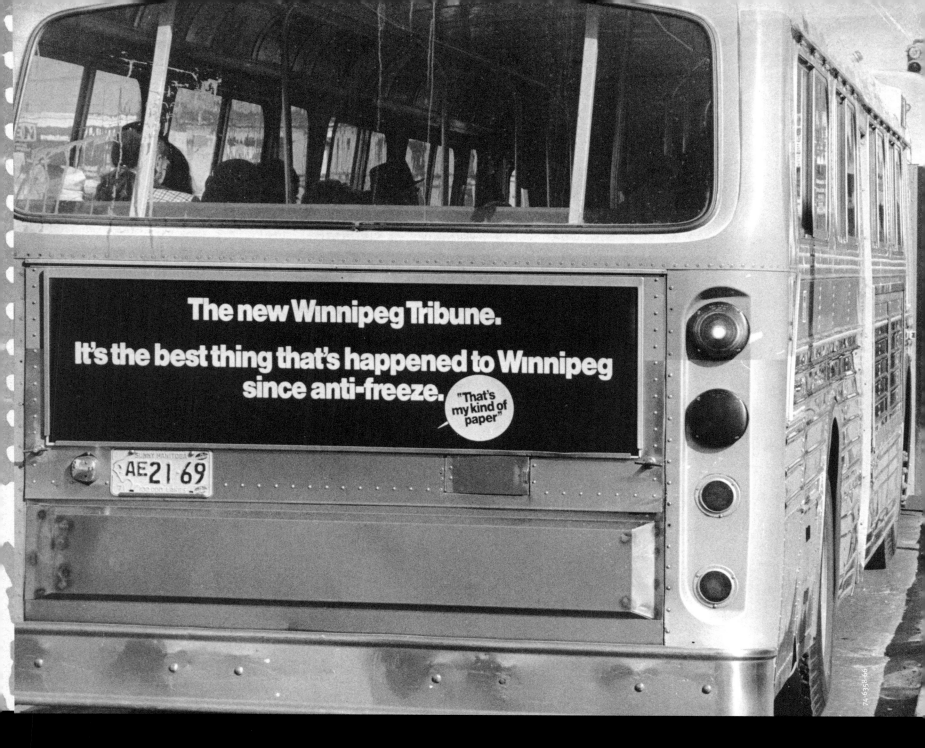

To safeguard the secrecy of The Trib's campaign, bus signs were hidden in the garage of advertising director Norm Weitzel's Westwood-area home until the time came to mount them on buses.

BLOCKBUSTER BILLBOARD

In March, 1977, the Trib displayed what it described as a "blockbuster billboard," atop the historic five-storey Casa Loma Building at the corner of Portage and Sherbrook. Measuring more than 23 feet high and 60 feet across (compared to a conventional billboard's 12 feet by 40 feet) with a 13-foot letter "T", it incorporated more than 4,200 light bulbs to maximize its visibility after dark.

Photo courtesy Gerry Haslam

The "old" and the "new" *Tribune* in 1975.

Veteran journalist Val Werier points out that competition was usually tempered with a spirit of co-operation. He describes it a "collegial convention where you helped people in opposition. If a newcomer came on the beat you sort of showed him around." One *Free Press* reporter at city hall wasn't helpful when young Werier first arrived there, but he was able to identify which offices the other reporter had already visited by tracking the scent of his aromatic Irish pipe tobacco. With a reporter's talent for detail, Werier recalls that the reporter smoked Erinmore Mixture.

Sportswriter Ed Dearden describes the rivalry by explaining "We got along as colleagues, but we were always out to try to beat one another."

Dearden remembers one night in 1971 when Vic Grant arrived in the newsroom around midnight and proudly announced that he had a scoop for the front page of the sports section: "Bobby Hull is coming to Winnipeg!" Dearden's first response was "Vic, go have another drink," but Grant insisted that he knew Ben Hatskin well and that the hockey legend would soon be joining the Jets. Grant wrote the story, it ran – scooping the *Free Press* – and, as Dearden recalls, "It was history in the making."

In the forthright style familiar to generations of Manitoba sports fans, Jack Matheson reflects, "We were always able to beat them in the sport department – probably because we tried a little harder. We beat the Freep in football coverage, in hockey coverage, in curling coverage, in golf coverage."

The Re-launch of *The Tribune*

According to Gerry Haslam, it was A. Ron Williams who decided to persuade Southam to invest enough money in *The Tribune* to "really take on the *Free Press*." Haslam was the managing editor in 1974, and Williams was the publisher. *Free Press* circulation was in the vicinity of 100,000, while the Trib's was only around half of that. For some time, *Free Press* ads had been boasting "In Winnipeg it's the *Free Press* two to one" — a slogan virtually begging for a fight.

A comprehensive marketing survey of Manitobans revealed that *The Tribune* needed improvement in a number of areas: classified ads, layout, editorials, and promotion. Haslam and Williams visited newspapers across Canada and in the U.S., and considerable brainstorming took place in Toronto and in Winnipeg.

The result was a $240,000 13-week campaign to acquaint Manitobans with "The New *Winnipeg Tribune*." beginning with the September 6, 1975 issue, *The Tribune* underwent a complete redesign, including a dramatic new yellow masthead and a modular layout system that saw lengthy front page stories consistently carried over to page five. To provide more community news coverage, the newsroom staff jumped

CONCEIVED IN SECRECY

Planning for *The Tribune's* dramatic re-launch in 1975 was an exercise in covert strategy. Only a handful of people within *The Tribune*, the Southam head office, and the Toronto advertising agency Vickers and Benson were aware of the project. When representatives flew between Winnipeg and Toronto for meetings, they took different flights at different times, never travelling as a group. Ads for the campaign were booked from different cities and not in the name of *The Winnipeg Tribune*. The code name of "lifestyle" was used for bookings, as was the more transparent "enubirt."

from 72 to 84. There were billboards, bus ads, radio spots, t-shirts, and buttons, all heralding an exciting new beginning for *The Tribune*.

But the innovation that attracted everyone's attention was that *The Tribune* was offering free private-party want ads. Haslam recalls that as many as a thousand free ads were booked each day - and, of course, some commercial advertisers found ways of getting their ads in the classifieds for free. The radical idea caught the attention of newspaper people across North America. Some labelled it "insane."

Advertising director Norm Weitzel explains that prior to the re-launch, the *Free Press's* classified advertising rates, despite its higher circulation, were actually lower than *The Tribune's*, an obvious tactic to undercut the competition. *The Tribune's* free classifieds strategy, along with expanded news coverage, increased and lower-priced commercial advertising, and gratifying growth in circulation resulted in the need to print more copies of larger newspapers. The sheer volume of these welcome developments placed increasing pressure on *The Tribune's*

aging presses and began to raise concerns about *The Tribune's* ability to sustain its newly gained growth. Weitzel sums up the eventual irony of the situation by saying "Our success became the main reason for our demise."

In mid-1975, *The Tribune's* circulation was 69,000, compared to the *Free Press's* 136,000. By March, 1976, the Trib's circulation had jumped to 86,000, and by the summer of 1976, the Free Press had taken down the signs that trumpeted their two-to-one dominance. An article in the February, 1979 issue of *Enterprise in Manitoba* listed early-1979 figures of 104,000 for *The Tribune* and 106,000 for the *Free Press* and proclaimed "The underdog is no more."

Some sources have suggested that *Tribune* circulation had caught up to or even exceeded the circulation of the *Free Press* in the first six months of 1980. Unfortunately, even if those reports are accurate, the cost of the sprint to catch its competitor was more than *The Tribune* (or at least its parent company) could sustain.

A key element of the re-launch was free want ads.

(left to right) Reporters
John Drabble, Carol Picard,
and editor Mike Flynn in
the news room (1979)

Rumblings that *The Tribune* would close had circulated intermittently for decades, but in 1980 there were reasons to be optimistic. The "New Tribune" had caught the imagination of Manitobans and, for the first time ever, there were rumours that dared to suggest that *The Tribune* had become number one.

Black Wednesday

The Announcement

Trib Magazine Editor Buzz Currie knew something was wrong when he couldn't feel the vibration of the presses through the floor. Editorial cartoonist Jan Kamienski remembers seeing Southam president Gordon Fisher standing on the news editor's desk as he walked into the newsroom. Photographer Jeff De Booy couldn't believe what he was hearing, and remembers seeing a colleague sobbing, running down the stairs. Legislative columnist Frances Russell had a phone call at home from a friend, telling her the bad news. Sports writer Ed Dearden found out the next day when he phoned home from Halifax, where he was covering the Canadian Golf Championships.

The Tribune was closing. It was Wednesday, August 27, 1980. Tribbers came to call it "Black Wednesday."

Editor Dona Harvey and other Trib senior management people had been summoned to a special meeting with head office people on the Tuesday evening in a private room at the Winnipeg Inn.

"We met until well after midnight planning how we would tell staff, how we would announce it to the public," she recalls. Southam president Gordon Fisher offered to break the sad news to the staff, and they agreed it would happen at a meeting at 9:00 the next morning.

The Tuesday evening meeting ended after midnight, and Harvey went home to write the front page story for the last issue. "How could I have given it to anyone else to write?" she asks rhetorically. She was particularly concerned about one member of the editorial staff, who was recuperating from a massive heart attack, and tracked down his doctor to ask if he could take the shock of the news. The doctor said he thought the man could handle it.

Early the next morning, Harvey left for work, but on the way she stopped by the home of the editor who had had a heart attack and told him the news. Around 8:30 a.m. she told staff members there would be a meeting at 9:00.

Al Hutchinson was on his way home to bed early Wednesday morning following his usual overnight shift in the composing room. "I should have known something was happening when the production manager and the controller were walking through the parking lot at seven o'clock in the morning." Hutchinson's wife later heard about the closing on Peter Warren's CJOB talk show, but she didn't wake him up to tell him.

Dona Harvey relives the 9:00 scene. "There were several hundred people crowded into the newsroom. Fisher started to speak, but it was hard for people to hear and see him, so I suggested he get up on a desk. That's now a classic photo. He stood up and said to everyone, 'This was my decision.'"

The Shock

The closing of *The Tribune* left about 650 people suddenly jobless. Columnist Marjorie Earl was three years from retirement. Val Werier was 61, and so was outdoor columnist Kit Kitney. Kitney had been at the Trib for 35 years.

Gene Telpner reflected on the new office furnishings for his office and wondered about the new drapes that had been ordered. Buzz Currie remembers feeling "a sense of elation because you didn't have to get a paper out the next day."

Many of the staffers went to the nearby Press Club as soon as they left the building. Some later went from there to photo editor Frank Chalmers' house. Photographer Jon Thordarson remembers, "We went down to the Press Club and drank so much, but couldn't get drunk. Beer after beer after beer — we just sat there stunned." Columnist Frances Russell describes the mood as a kind of bravura during a state of shock. "Everybody was laughing and sort of crying, and laughing and crying." Some *Free Press* staffers joined the Tribbers at the Press Club to commiserate. Competition was fine, but these were fellow newspaper people who had just lost their jobs.

JACK MATHESON

"We knew pretty well what was coming when we saw these suits from down east. Bob Irving at CJOB got wind of our demise and phoned my home to commiserate. He got my wife out of bed, saying he was sorry to hear about my bad news. My wife immediately thought the worst, that I'd been wiped out in a car accident or something like that and she shouted, 'What's happened? What's happened, Bob?' At this point he realized she didn't have the faintest idea what he was talking about so he told her then and there. 'The Trib,' he said gravely, 'has folded.' And my dear wife was so suitably relieved she said 'Oh, is that all?' I got home half an hour later and gave her all the gruesome details."

JAN KAMIENSKI

"Somebody from the management announced that only personal items could be taken out of the building. Anything else must stay. We were so closely woven into that Tribune existing system, that ours was *The Tribune's* property and *The Tribune's* was our property, and Goddamn it, we were not going to let it go. I had a stack of cartoons about a metre high, all originals, and I had just as many at home, and I took them out. There was some flunky downstairs, a security guard, who was looking daggers at me, and I said, 'These are my cartoons, my property, not the property of *The Tribune*.' Telpner took his typewriter, I should say *The Tribune's* typewriter, with him through the back door."

The Tribune's
FINANCIAL LOSSES
GERRY HASLAM

"One of the interesting things about all of this was that I was the managing editor at the time of the re-launch and I was subsequently the editor of the paper, and I never, ever once saw the financial statements. So I never knew how much money we were losing. But I know now we were losing a fair chunk of money, and in the end that's why the paper was closed."

The newsroom in 1979

The Rationale and the Reflections

The Winnipeg Tribune was closed as the result of an agreement between two newspaper chains.

Thomson Newspapers closed the *Ottawa Journal* on August 26th, 1980. Southam Inc. closed *The Winnipeg Tribune* the next day and sold its assets to the *Free Press* for $2.2 million. Thomson's *Vancouver Sun* became a Southam newspaper and, at the same time, Thomson sold its interests in Pacific Press Ltd. of Vancouver and Gazette-Montreal Ltd. to Southam for a total of $57.25 million.

Much of the local anger at the time, particularly among the more than 100,000 subscribers of *The Tribune*, was aimed at this "board room deal." The fact that the agreement was made in Toronto helped bring in Winnipeggers' typical resentment of "down east" doings.

The reality is that, in its last brave effort to win its ninety-year contest with the *Free Press*, *The Tribune* had, with the blessing of Southam, committed financial suicide.

Most estimates of the Trib's losses in its last five years of operation are in the area of $16 million. As the last editor, Dona Harvey was aware that *The Tribune* was losing about five million a year. Jack Matheson sums up *The Tribune's* final attempt to become the leading newspaper, "We didn't want to be a nice comfortable number two. We didn't want to play it that way. We wanted number one and we didn't get it."

Dona Harvey points out that Manitoba was entering a recession in 1980, and recessions are always hard on second-place newspapers.

As advertising budgets are trimmed, only the leading newspapers get the ads.

Some Tribbers speculate, perhaps as an exercise in retroactive wishful thinking, that it could have been the *Free Press* that went under instead of *The Tribune*. Some wonder if a major factor was the presses – *The Tribune's* were old and in need of replacement, and that price tag was around $25 million.

Knowledgeable newspaper people point out that markets the size of Winnipeg simply can't support two major daily newspapers. In a *Free Press* story on the day of the closure, Gordon Fisher was quoted as saying, "In the final analysis, we have concluded that Winnipeg is a market that will not support two viable daily newspapers. ...our directors are certain that our success would be contingent on the demise of our competitor, the *Free Press*. In either case, Winnipeg would lose one of its traditional newspapers."

The Arrangements

In a memo to all employees, publisher E. H. (Bill) Wheatley outlined the termination provisions. Regular employees were to receive their full pay until the end of 1980, with all benefits except long term disability insurance to continue for the same period at company expense. In addition, severance pay would be calculated on the basis of one week's pay for each six months of service.

WINNIPEG AS A TWO-NEWSPAPER CITY
DONA HARVEY

"*The Tribune* and the *Ottawa Journal* helped clarify that it was impossible in a city of around half a million to run two all-purpose daily newspapers head-to-head. Economically you couldn't do it. The nature of advertising, the size of the community – you just could not have two broad circulation newspapers. We didn't know that. I don't think anybody did."

All Southam subsidiaries were informed of the closure of *The Tribune* in case they had job opportunities for Trib employees. A personnel committee was formed to help employees find new employment, and job opportunities were posted in the main floor lobby.

Although a considerable number of ex-Tribbers were eventually employed by Southam in other Canadian cities, the prospect of leaving Winnipeg was a problem for some. Al Hutchinson was offered a position with the *Edmonton Journal* but, as he explains, "I was 47 years old and had three teenagers. I didn't want to uproot them." Jack Matheson was also offered a job by Southam with the *Edmonton Journal*, but his son worked there and "I don't think it would have been a good idea to have two of us on one staff."

Within five minutes of the announcement, Dona Harvey recalls, the office phones began to ring. "There were newspapers and other organizations – businesses – with job offers from across the country. It was just phenomenal! You have no idea what a sense of relief and hope that provided everyone, even though the effect of the closure was devastating."

The Aftermath

Over the years, *The Winnipeg Tribune* had built up a team of very capable people, and it's not surprising that, after the initial shock of joblessness, many landed on their feet and still in Winnipeg. Vic Grant, Ed Dearden, Eric Wells, and Peter Warren moved to radio. Others, perhaps after a side trip or two, went to the *Free Press*, including Val Werier, Buzz Currie, Frances Russell, and photographers Jon Thordarson and Jeff De Booy. Some were involved in founding the *Winnipeg Sun* or joined its staff, including Frank Chalmers, Buzz Currie, Kelly Armstrong, and Jan Kamienski. Peter Liba established a new career in broadcasting and went on to become the Lieutenant Governor of Manitoba. Others accepted offers from Southam to move to newspapers in other cities; some found jobs in different fields of work; some retired.

There were reunions on the anniversary of "Black Wednesday" for the first couple of years, but by then the Tribbers had forged new lives and moved on.

But that doesn't mean they've forgotten the Trib, their experiences together, or each other. Al Hutchinson, who spent from 1952 to 1980 in the composing room, sums it up. "I had the best job in the world. I miss it. I really do. I miss all the people."

TAKING NO CHANCES

The management of the *Free Press* in 1980 might have been aware that *The Tribune* was able to get started in 1890 by taking over the building and equipment of a newspaper that had been absorbed by the *Free Press*. Or perhaps they were just more cautious than their predecessors. In either case, the *Free Press* acquired *The Tribune's* building, its equipment, and its name, effectively ensuring that no upstart publication could move into the Smith and Graham premises or use the name of *The Winnipeg Tribune*. The building was demolished in 1983 and replaced by a parking lot. The name of *The Winnipeg Tribune* continues to appear on the editorial page of every issue of the *Free Press*, right next to that paper's own name. The strategy makes it clear that *The Tribune's* name is the property of the *Free Press*. It could also be interpreted to mean that each issue of the *Winnipeg Free Press* is also an issue of *The Winnipeg Tribune*.

The Tribune has left legacies to the people of Manitoba that will outlive the individuals who created the newspaper and those who used to read it. The Trib set a standard in writing and photography that continues to be a benchmark. And, as a chronicle of life in Manitoba for nine decades, *The Tribune* left a collection of words and images that provide a fascinating and increasingly valuable record of the times.

Legacies of
The Tribune

A Legacy of Honest Coverage and Dedication to Craft

In the ninety years that *The Winnipeg Tribune* informed and entertained Manitobans, it made an indelible mark on the history of the province.

For most of its years, the Trib, as a daily newspaper serving a city and a province, had only one competitor. The continuous competition between the two rivals served to improve the quality of both. Knowing that Manitobans had a choice motivated the editors, journalists, and photographers of both *The Tribune* and the *Free Press* to produce the best product they could create. Gerry Haslam recalls from his days as editor, "Every time the *Free Press* had a story that we didn't have, the publisher used to summon me to his office and – quite pleasantly – yell at me."

The Tribune's self-imposed mandate to cover the local scene meant that Manitobans learned more about events across their province. Gregg Burner recalls that, as a Trib photographer, he had opportunities to spend entire days at rural community events like the Dauphin Ukrainian Festival and the Morden Corn and Apple Festival, and that the photos he shot there were usually published.

The Tribune was both a training ground and a haven for some of the best media people in Canada. On the national scene, such notables as Ralph Allen, Ken Black, Jim Coleman, Robert Cross, Lindsay Crysler, Peter Desbarats, Robert Hunter, Don Newman, Roger Newman, Martin O'Malley, Randolph Patton, Heather Robertson, and Robert Taylor are examples of journalists whose craft was shaped by *The Tribune*.

Russ Gourluck photos

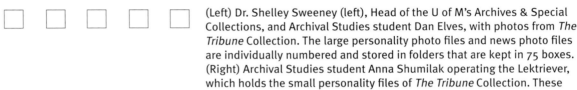

(Left) Dr. Shelley Sweeney (left), Head of the U of M's Archives & Special Collections, and Archival Studies student Dan Elves, with photos from *The Tribune* Collection. The large personality photo files and news photo files are individually numbered and stored in folders that are kept in 75 boxes. (Right) Archival Studies student Anna Shumilak operating the Lektriever, which holds the small personality files of *The Tribune* Collection. These files include photos and clippings about thousands of individuals.

The Tribune, many former employees recall, stressed quality. Buzz Currie remembers the Trib's attention to writing, describing it as "an editors' newspaper." Jim Shilliday values the newspaper's "serious and ethical attitude" and its "pervasive dedication to craft." Peter Warren believes that *The Tribune* "left a legacy of honest coverage."

Many Manitobans would agree with Jan Kamienski's observation that *The Tribune* was "a newspaper with a social conscience. It had a conscience that emanated from the management."

The words of Jack Matheson, never known to pull a journalistic punch, reveal the pride that Tribbers had in what they did: "We left behind a hell of a product. I was so proud. I thought we had the best paper in Canada."

A Legacy of Information

Beginning in the late 1930s, *The Tribune* accumulated an extensive collection of clippings, files, and photographs. Shortly after the paper folded, Dona Harvey and officials of Thomson Newspapers, the *Free Press*, and the University of Manitoba began arranging to have these "morgue files" transferred to the department of Archives & Special Collections of the University Libraries. Funding for the move was provided by The Winnipeg Foundation. For the traditional token sum of one dollar, the University of Manitoba became the owner and caretakers of the collection.

It was a huge undertaking. Part of the deal was a massive electrical-mechanical device known as a Lektriever, a series of moving horizontal shelves that house files and allow for relatively easy retrieval. This mechanical forerunner of Google needed to be carefully dismantled at The *Tribune* Building and then reassembled at the University. Because of the sheer size and weight of the materials (243 metres or 266 yards, and 8 tons), structural tests of the bearing capacity of the floors and renovations of the storage vaults were needed. The collection officially opened on June 19, 1981.

The *Tribune* Collection includes approximately 2,500,000 clippings in more than 11,000 subject categories and 60,000 personality files, as well as approximately 250,000 photographs. The original 350-page index, typewritten by *Tribune* staff, is intact and available for use. Most of the subject files have been preserved on 167 reels of microfilm.

The *Tribune* Collection is a priceless source of information on Manitoba and Canadian history from 1935 to 1980. High quality photographs taken by *Tribune* staff photographers provide glimpses of life in Manitoba, particularly from the 1950s to 1980, and form the basis of the second part of this book.

The collection is accessible to the public.

The Tribune published an extra edition for VE Day in May, 1945 when the war ended in Europe. Standing left to right: publisher Dr. Wesley McCurdy; editor John Bird; business manager Arthur W. Moscarella; recently-returned war correspondent Richard L. Sanburn; circulation manager Sam Sigesmund. Seated at desk left to right: news editor Carlyle Allison; desk man Nate Zimmerman; slot man John M. Gordon; desk man Fred Johnson; columnist Victor V. Murray; desk man Bill Good

For ninety years, the journalists of *The Winnipeg Tribune* became part of thousands of Manitoba households as their work was seen and discussed by countless family members. Many Tribbers, and particularly the regular columnists, created the kind of kinships readers feel for writers whose work strikes sympathetic chords. The following is a retrospective on some of the people whose personalities shaped the identity of *The Winnipeg Tribune*.

The Personalities

Carlyle Allison

Carlyle Allison, a graduate of the University of Manitoba, first worked for *The Winnipeg Tribune* in 1926. After gaining experience with newspapers in Saskatoon and Montreal, Allison returned to *The Tribune* in 1935 and was appointed editor-in-chief in 1946. In 1951, he began writing a column titled "The Corner Cupboard" that was printed on the editorial page each Saturday for a number of years. A collection of these

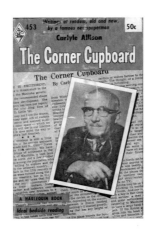

columns was published by Harlequin in 1958 in a book bearing the same name.

Buzz Currie

Buzz Currie began with *The Tribune* as an older-than-average copy boy in the fall of 1970. "I was pretty old when I started as a copy boy. I think I was 22," he recalls. With only two non-smokers in an editorial department of close to a hundred, much of his time in that job was spent going out to buy cigarettes for staffers.

By early 1971, Currie had become a reporter, beginning with the night police beat, then covering council meetings of the various municipalities that made up Winnipeg at the time. He had no formal journalism training, but thought "writing would be a good thing to do."

66-6358-173

COPY BOYS

When "COPY!" was shouted in the newsroom, a copy boy came running. Although
the origin of the practice was to summon one of the very junior employees to deliver
reporters' copy sheets (folded pieces of newsprint on which stories were typed) to the
composing room, its purpose broadened to encompass virtually any kind of errand.
Often a lad who responded to "COPY!" found himself bringing back coffee (which, in the
pre-styrofoam era was often carried in red cardboard cartons of emptied Coke bottles).
Becoming a copy boy was often an entry-level position that led to becoming a reporter. In
the meantime, a copy boy essentially did all of the menial jobs in the newsroom that no
one else wanted to do.

66-6358-206

(Right) The newsroom in 1957;
(Below) The newsroom in 1961

74-6358-168

The newsroom in 1967

74-6358-141

74-6358-199

(Above) Left to right: Ray Moscarella (advertising director) A. Ron Williams (publisher) Tom Green (editor-in-chief) Gordon Aikman (photo editor) Dick Hawkins (composing room superintendent) (1967)

(Left) An editorial conference in 1950. Left to right: editorial writer Fred Johnson; associate editor Randolph Patton; executive editor Fred O'Malley; editor Carlyle Allison; associate editor Tom Green; cartoonist Ed McGibbon.

 Ed Dearden (1965).

Eventually he moved on to the Legislative bureau and later become city editor. At the time *The Tribune* folded, Currie was editing the magazine section.

Currie recalls the camaraderie of *The Tribune*, including the after-work sessions at the St. Regis Hotel bar, and reflects, "It was almost like a home. It was your social life and everything all rolled into one."

Buzz Currie stayed on the Southam payroll until the summer of 1981, and, in the meantime, along with fellow *Tribune* alumni Kelly Armstrong and Frank Chalmers, helped establish the *Winnipeg Sun*. Currie is now a member of the editorial staff of the *Winnipeg Free Press* and co-authored the best-selling book *The Hermetic Code*.

Ed Dearden

Ed Dearden describes himself as a "*Tribune* lifer". As a boy, he was a delivery helper, but the person who had the route let him go just before Christmas to avoid sharing the tips. In 1944, when Dearden was looking for a career as a tradesman, Vince Leah got him a job as an apprentice printer in the composing room at $11 a week. That job lasted until a 1945 strike hit both newspapers, so Dearden began working for the CPR. In 1952, "Uncle Vince" offered him another job – answering the phones in *The Tribune* Sports department for $5.00 a night to copy down sports scores, and this led to the chance to do some writing. Dearden continued working for the railway full time and freelancing for *The Tribune* until 1959, when he became a full-time sports writer. In 1965 he was named assistant sports editor. Initially Dearden's main beat was golf, but in the mid-1970s he became *The Tribune's* principal writer for the WHA Jets, as well as a colour commentator for Ken Nicolson on CJOB's Jets broadcasts. In 1976, he covered the Jets in Moscow, and a year later Dearden (accompanied by Nicolson) was the only print journalist from Winnipeg who made the journey to Tokyo to report on the three games the Jets played against the Soviet national team. During the summer, Dearden also did golf reports on CJOB.

Looking back on their years together with *The Tribune*, sports editor Jack Matheson gives much of the credit for his own success to Dearden. "Steady Eddie Dearden was my strong right arm. I wouldn't have been anything without him."

Ed Dearden was named to the Manitoba Golfing Hall of Fame in 2007.

Lillian Gibbons

Lillian Gibbons, born in Winnipeg in 1906, was undoubtedly one of the most eccentric individuals ever to be on the staff of *The Winnipeg Tribune*. Tiny and sparrow-like in appearance, she wore brightly coloured wool suits year-round, along with platform heels, dainty gloves, and conspicuous wide-brimmed hats that she purchased at second hand stores. Gibbons was notoriously frugal, living alone in the same tiny Smith Street apartment, crammed with books and papers, for sixty years.

Her writing style clashed with standard newspaper expectations. As Val Werier discreetly puts it, "she was a problem for city editors." Jim Shilliday, who also had to edit her work, describes her approach as "stream of consciousness, not inverted pyramid", explaining that she'd start her stories with whatever she recalled first. "We always read her stuff right to the end because sometimes down near the very bottom there'd be an outrageous remark someone made. Either we would rewrite her story, bringing that up to the top, making it sort of in the semblance of *Tribune* style, or we'd put another reporter on it, saying, 'Go and check this out'." Shilliday adds, "She couldn't write a story, but she was marvellous at picking out details of things that were interesting or significant."

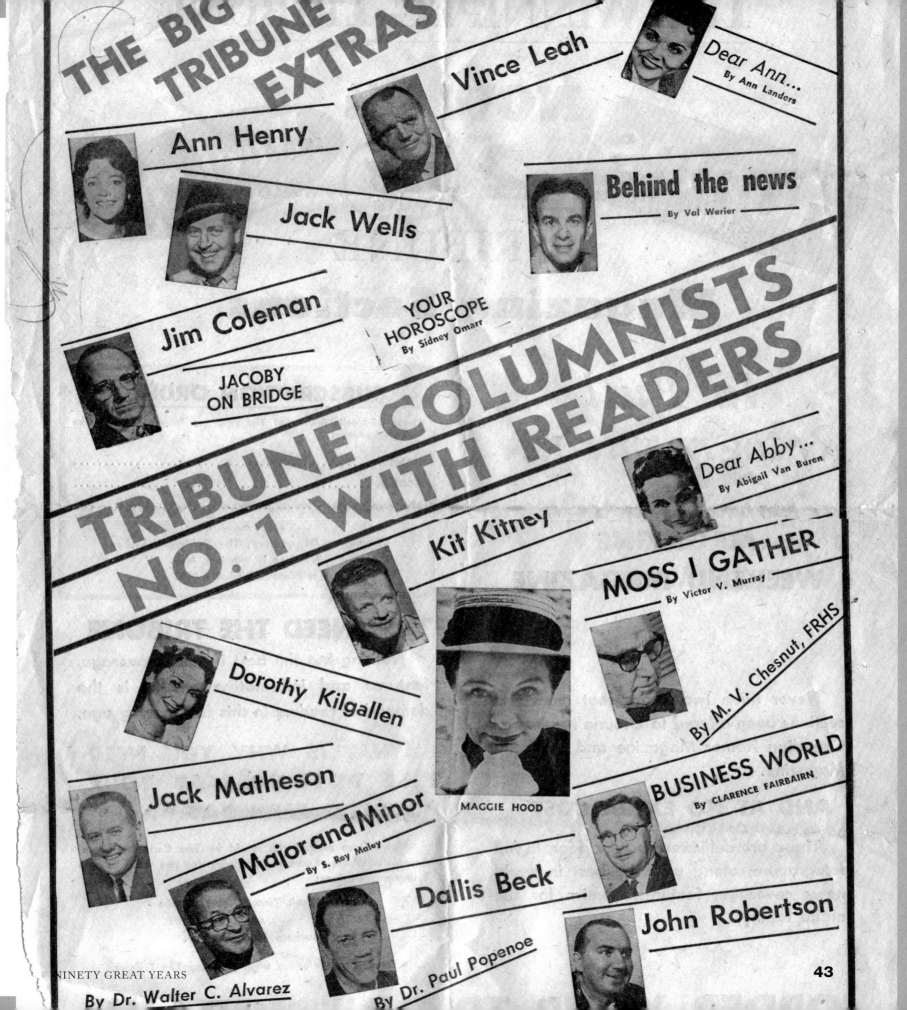

THE BIG TRIBUNE EXTRAS

TRIBUNE COLUMNISTS NO. 1 WITH READERS

Vince Leah

Dear Ann...
By Ann Landers

Ann Henry

Behind the news
By Val Werier

Jack Wells

Jim Coleman

YOUR HOROSCOPE
By Sidney Omarr

JACOBY ON BRIDGE

Dear Abby...
By Abigail Van Buren

Kit Kitney

MOSS I GATHER
By Victor V. Murray

By M. V. Chesnut, FRHS

Dorothy Kilgallen

BUSINESS WORLD
By CLARENCE FAIRBAIRN

Jack Matheson

MAGGIE HOOD

Major and Minor
By S. Roy Maley

Dallis Beck

John Robertson

By Dr. Walter C. Alvarez

By Dr. Paul Popenoe

LEGENDS OF LILLIAN GIBBONS

Most Tribbers who worked with Lillian Gibbons have favourite stories to tell about their eccentric colleague. Some of the tales have undoubtedly been stretched by repeated tellings and the passage of time.

One story tells how Gibbons was, as part of her "hotels, rails, and clubs" assignment, covering the departure of troops leaving by train for Europe during World War II5. Noting that some of the railway cars were covered with graffiti that used the crudest possible language to describe the Nazis, she carefully wrote the slogans down verbatim and included them in the story she submitted. The editors were horrified and, of course, deleted the offensive language. The tellers of this story aren't sure if Gibbons was really that naïve, or was simply testing her editors.

Another story is told by Jim Shilliday. One summer day, when he, Hugh Allan, and Lillian Gibbons were driving to an assignment, Gibbons asked if they could stop by her downtown apartment to pick something up. When they arrived there, she invited them to come up to her suite and hospitably offered them a drink of beer. Gibbons emerged from the tiny kitchen with a single, previously opened bottle of beer and carefully poured an ounce into a shot glass for each man. Shilliday describes the beer as "totally flat", but remembers that he and Allan did their best to appear to savour each sip.

Lillian Gibbons' frugality is often illustrated by her habit of cramming her large and ever-present handbag with leftover buns from the luncheons she regularly attended. Her eccentricity is demonstrated by the fact that, before she sat on an office chair that was shared with other employees, she carefully laid out blank copy paper on the seat.

Lillian Gibbons, shown at her desk in 1971, was known by many for her distinctive hats and eccentric ways. Fewer recognized her extensive talents.

Frank Chalmers photo 1018-6

Vic Grant recalls that, in 1979, rumours began circulating in Winnipeg that Molson's Brewery, as a World Hockey Association team owner, was opposed to the entry of the Winnipeg Jets into the National Hockey League. Grant's logic was straightforward: "If Molson's is going to vote against Winnipeg and not want to do business with Winnipeg, why should Winnipeg want to do any business with Molson's? So I did this protest for a moratorium on buying Molson's beer. Molson's pulled in their horns."

Jon Thordarson photo

Many of her colleagues (including some editors) believed that her job at *The Tribune* was secured by a large amount of Southam stock she was reputed to own, but others insist that her shares in the company were minimal. For years Gibbons was assigned "the lunch circuit" or "hotels, rails, and clubs." This meant that much of her time was spent attending luncheons of service clubs and other innocuous groups and writing stories that were often thrown in a wastebasket.

Sometimes Gibbons was assigned miscellaneous duties, just to keep her busy. Peter Warren tells how he tasked Gibbons with finding him a rolltop desk. One day she burst into his office, saying "Give me fifty dollars! I found it!" She had located a "gorgeous" desk in the basement of the Grain Exchange Building. A *Tribune* truck picked it up, and Warren, who still has it, says it's now valued at $15,000 to $20,000.

Lillian Gibbons, one of the first women in Manitoba to work in a daily newspaper, graduated from the University of Manitoba in 1928 as a gold medalist, and returned a few years later to receive her master's degree in history. She wrote numerous articles for the Manitoba Historical Society and had two books published. The first, rather oddly titled considering the author, was *My Love Affair with Louis Riel* (1969). The next, *Stories Houses Tell* (1978), was based on a series she began in *The Tribune* in 1935, and it became a best seller. Frances Russell remembers Lillian Gibbons as "a very, very bright woman."

Despite her quiet and frugal lifestyle, Lillian Gibbons undertook adventurous annual trips. Her final excursion, in 1996 at the age of 89, was on the Amazon River in Brazil. Perhaps sensing that her death was near, she instructed her fellow travellers to throw her body overboard if she died on the boat. She did die there, but she was accorded a much more traditional service in Winnipeg. Lillian Gibbons' estate of half a million dollars, the result of productive stock market investments, was left to her favourite charities.

Vic Grant

Vic Grant's journalism career began in 1964 when he walked into Jack Matheson's office and said "I want to be a sports writer." Matheson started him off in the usual way, as a copy boy, and within six months Grant was assigned to writing sports. Like many of his contemporaries, Vic Grant had no formal training in journalism. He was sent to a smaller Southam paper to broaden his experience, and when he returned to *The Tribune*, his wages were tripled.

As a sports writer, Vic Grant covered hockey at various levels, becoming *The Tribune's* primary hockey reporter when the WHA started up in 1972. At the same time, CJOB recruited Grant to do the colour commentary for WHA games. While he was in Russia in 1974 to cover the Canada-Russia series, he wrote a series of articles on Russia and the Russian perspective of life, which were printed by Southam papers across Canada. When Grant returned to Winnipeg, publisher Ron Williams pulled him out of sports and made him an editorial columnist. Vic Grant wrote provocative and controversial columns until *The Tribune* closed in 1980.

Grant's explanation for the change of assignment is characteristically forthright – he says he was considered a 'shit-disturber'. Editor Gerry Haslam's rationale is more strategic. "We moved him from covering the Winnipeg Jets to being a general columnist because Williams believed that a star columnist could turn around the fortunes of a newspaper. He was supposed to be controversial, and he was." And Dona Harvey sums up Grant in just a few words. "Vic has a gift of understanding Winnipeg and speaking it plainly."

After *The Tribune* folded, Vic Grant went to Calgary, where he was a consultant for Southam. Vic Grant joined radio station CJOB in 1989, and is currently the station's news and program director. His daily commentary, titled "Excuse Me," is, as might be expected, provocative and controversial.

Tom Green

After editor Eric Wells unexpectedly left *The Tribune* in the late 1960s, he was succeeded by Tom Green. Green was a long-time editorial writer who had risen through the ranks, and was then called on to fill the vacancy created by Wells's departure. A quiet and reserved man, Green maintained a low profile as editor.

A standing inside joke during that era was that three of the top people at *The Tribune* were Tom, Dick, and Harry – Tom Green, Dick Goodwin, and Harry Mardon.

Dona Harvey

When Dona (pronounced "Donna") Harvey, barely into her thirties, was appointed managing editor of *The Winnipeg Tribune* in 1976 she became the first woman ever to hold that position in a metropolitan daily newspaper in Canada. After Gerry Haslam left *The Tribune* the following year, Harvey became the editor-in-chief.

REFLECTIONS ON DONA HARVEY'S TENURE AS *The Tribune's* FIRST FEMALE NEWSPAPER EDITOR

"She was going into a den with a bunch of crusty old guys that she had to manage. More people wanted her to fail than to succeed. There was definitely a glass ceiling there. (Gregg Burner, photographer)

"Looking back, I think she was our best editor." (Jack Matheson, sports editor)

"One of the things about working in a newsroom is that what you do every day is there for everyone to see. If you are capable and do well, others will notice. And if you botch up, that will become known pretty quickly too. And so there's a culture in a newsroom of granting people respect if they earn it and deserve it. It doesn't matter so much if they're male or female." (Dona Harvey)

Asked about the reactions of her colleagues when she was first hired for a job traditionally occupied by males, Harvey recalls, "On the whole, it was a very warm reception. There were a few people who held back and needed me to be able to prove myself. Over the course of time, fortunately, I think I was able to do that for most of them."

Regina-born Harvey says she's been in newspapering all of her life, beginning as a reporter at the age of sixteen in the state of Washington, then working as a reporter in Edmonton.

After handling the cheerless task of closing down *The Winnipeg Tribune*, Harvey was managing editor of Southam's *Vancouver Province*, spent some time in Jerusalem (her husband is a theology professor), then became an Assistant Vice-President at the University of Toronto. As this book went to press in 2008, Dona Harvey was living in Waterloo, Ontario.

DELAYED DELIVERIES

Gerry Haslam remembers the time that Vic Grant decided to write a piece about the out-call massage business, which was really a service to chauffeur prostitutes to their customers. To add to the authenticity of his story, Grant managed to wangle a job as a driver for one of the services. Armed with a Chargex machine, he drove the women to various destinations across the city – often hotels – then picked them up later to go on to their next appointment. Haslam recalls that when he read the column, which was "clearly about sex", he decided to run it on an inside page rather than the front page. A front page "teaser" advised readers what Grant's story was about and included a caution that the material might not be suitable for some readers. "That," Haslam acknowledges, "was a big mistake. The paper was delivered late all across the city that afternoon because virtually every carrier boy stopped and read the story before he started delivering his papers."

Gregg Burner photo 10629-1

HARVEY MEETS TRUDEAU

Gregg Burner remembers Dona Harvey's interview with Pierre Trudeau: "Somehow – I don't know how Dona did it – she wangled an interview with Trudeau. I went along and sat in on the interview. It was at the Fort Garry Hotel. One of the best things about being a photojournalist at the time was that on a good interview you could make excuses and stay and listen to the whole thing, and on a bad interview you could always leave like you had another assignment. I stuck around for the whole thing. He was loose with her, he wasn't as on guard. I put that copy of *The Tribune* there. In good photography, the triangles bring you into the faces. When I construct it properly, you will look at whatever I want you to look at and in the sequence I want you to look at it."

Dona Harvey interviewed Pierre Trudeau in 1977 about Canada's coming of age.

Frank Chalmers photo 10209-7

Gerry Haslam

Gerry Haslam arrived in Winnipeg in the summer of 1969 to work in radio, but his career path led to the *The Tribune*, where he eventually helped to spearhead the adventurous re-launch of the newspaper. He had previously lived in Ottawa, where he worked on Parliament Hill as an assistant to thirteen Conservative MP's, and later as an assistant to John Diefenbaker.

Initially Haslam was the successor to Bill Trebilcoe on radio station CKY's open-line show. The following year he was hired by CBC television (along with his counterpart from CJOB, John Harvard) to host *24 Hours*, a daily prime-time hour-long news and public affairs show. Each also did a radio show for CBC.

Having made his mark in Winnipeg radio and television, Haslam sent sample columns to the *Free Press* and *The Tribune*. His overture was rejected by the *Free Press*, but *Tribune* editor Tom Green asked him to write three columns a week at $25 per column. In the summer of 1972, Haslam joined *The Tribune* staff as a columnist and editorial writer, and after being rotated through various jobs to broaden his newspaper

(Below) Ann Henry – journalist, playwright, feminist (1954 photo) (Right) Jan Kamienski was The Trib's editorial cartoonist for more than two decades (1963 photo).

experience, was appointed managing editor in the fall of 1973. He was 28 years old.

Haslam remained with *The Tribune* until 1977 and was succeeded by Dona Harvey. After a brief stint in public relations with MacMillan Bloedel ("I realized that it was completely the wrong job for me."), Haslam returned to Southam where he became the publisher of both the *Vancouver Sun* and the *Vancouver Province*. He left Southam in 1992.

In 2008, Gerry Haslam was retired and living in British Columbia. Asked how he was spending his time, Haslam chuckled, "My dream was to become a rich and famous writer of novels. I've written two novels in my life, but neither one of them has seen the light of day."

Ann Henry

Ann Henry was much more than a columnist and a reviewer of movies for *The Tribune*. Frances Russell describes her as "one of the pioneers in Winnipeg for women in journalism."

A tribute paid to Henry in the Manitoba Legislature shortly after her death in 2000 at the age of 85 points out that she was the first woman reporter to cover the legislature and Winnipeg Police Courts and "the first woman assigned to cover hard news, at a fraction of

Ann Henry (1954)

the wages her male colleagues received." A single parent and a forthright feminist, she championed women's rights and promoted improved social services long before these became mainstream causes. Val Werier, who with Henry comprised a small left-wing contingent on the staff of *The Tribune*, describes her as "a real fighter for the underdog."

Ann Henry was a talented playwright, and *Lulu Street*, based on the 1919 Winnipeg General Strike, premiered at the Manitoba Theatre Centre in 1967, the first play written by a Manitoban about a Manitoba event to appear on Winnipeg's largest stage. Her legacy to theatre includes her two actor sons, Tim Henry and Donnelly Rhodes.

Jan Kamienski

Polish-born Jan (pronounced "Yan") Kamienski studied art at the Dresden Academy and in Paris before moving to Canada. After he and his wife arrived in Winnipeg in 1949, he worked as an illustrator in advertising art for a few years before becoming *The Tribune's* editorial cartoonist in 1958. In 1963, Kamienski received the coveted National Newspaper Award for editorial cartooning. His career with *The Tribune* continued until the paper closed in 1980.

His cartoons, drawn after attending daily editors' conferences where the news priorities for the following day were established, appeared six days a week (there was no Sunday edition). In addition, Kamienski wrote art reviews, edited the art page, and wrote a column appropriately titled "Now and Then" – "whenever I felt like it and on any subject I picked."

After *The Tribune* closed, Kamienski became the editorial cartoonist for the *Winnipeg Sun* until the paper was purchased by the Quebecor Group in 1983 and began using syndicated cartoons. The *Sun* published three volumes of his cartoons in three successive years. He donated 4,000 originals of his *Tribune* cartoons to the Archives of Manitoba.

FOR AN **INCENTIVE** SOCIETY

FOR A **JUST** SOCIETY

LEWIS

1972

"Hello? . . . 999?"

1961

Jan Kamienski's editorial cartoons offered graphic commentaries on local, national, and international issues. Kamienski believes that a cartoon needs to deliver a clear and immediate message. "A cartoon has to be as simple as possible and has to hit at the very first glance. If you have to wander around the cartoon and try to figure out the meaning, forget it. That's no cartoon."

NEWS ITEM:

RICHARD NIXON SAYS HE'S BEING PERSECUTED JUST AS ABRAHAM LINCOLN WAS.

1974

Uncle Vince sounds start SEP 27 1978 *p4*

The Trib's Vince Leah raises a pistol to start about 200 St. Paul's High School students and staff on a 15-mile walk Tuesday, to raise funds for studdent activities such as debating and sports. Organizers estimated they made about $6,000 in pledges, $2,000 more than expected. The student council gives five per cent of the funds to charity.

Vince Leah

Generations of Winnipeg kids knew him as "Uncle Vince, and even his colleagues referred to him as "Unk."" Vince Leah (pronounced "Lee") was an icon, both in his 63-year career as a journalist and as a member of the community.

Born in Winnipeg in 1913, 16-year-old Vince Leah began, like many of his newspaper contemporaries, as a copy boy, and he soon became a sports writer. His contributions to community sports included founding three hockey leagues as well as the Excelsior Hockey Club, but he also coached, managed, refereed, or promoted soccer, basketball, lacrosse, and baseball for youth. Leah is also credited with helping to bring Little League Baseball to Canada in 1959. Thousands of youngsters played sports with the help of Uncle Vince, and many went on to the professional level. Leah had a talent for wangling donations of sports equipment, jerseys, and equipment so that the kids in his programs didn't have to pay to participate.

As a *Tribune* columnist, Leah was primarily a sports writer, and is credited with naming the Winnipeg Blue Bombers (a variation on the "Brown Bomber" nickname of heavyweight boxing champ Joe Louis). He also achieved distinction as a writer of local nostalgia, telling timeless stories of people and events from earlier eras. After *The Tribune* closed, he was a columnist for the Free Press. Leah was the author of eight local history books, including a history of the Blue Bombers.

Vince Leah died in 1993, and his contributions have been honoured with the naming of two Winnipeg streets and a West Kildonan recreation centre after him. He was inducted into the Order of Canada, the Manitoba Sports Hall of Fame, and the Citizens Hall of Fame at Assiniboine Park. Uncle Vince's grey Underwood typewriter still sits in a corner of the *Free Press* newsroom, a silent reminder of a legendary journalist who left his mark on a community.

UNK'S TEETH

Vince Leah frequently exasperated his *Tribune* colleagues by leaving his dentures almost anywhere but in his mouth. As Jack Matheson recalls, "He used to leave his teeth in the drawer, and that used to scare everybody. They'd turn up in the damndest places." Gregg Burner was once given the task of shooting head-and-shoulders photos of all of the columnists, and remembers that the greatest challenge was "finding Unk with his teeth in."

VINCE LEAH'S GENEROSITY

Although Vince Leah's generosity with his time in promoting, coaching, managing, and refereeing sports for youngsters is legendary, his colleagues at *The Tribune* knew an ironically different side of his personality. He was notoriously frugal with his money. As Ed Dearden recalls, "he was always waiting for someone to buy him a coffee, buy him a lunch, treat him to a drink." Uncle Vince once bought Jim Shilliday a beer at the Press Club, and that was such a remarkable occasion that Shilliday remembers it more than forty years later. Leah was given a car at a tribute at the Amphitheatre Rink; it was the first car he'd ever owned, and he had to learn to drive.

Peter Liba

Described affectionately by Jack Matheson as *The Tribune's* "most famous copy boy," Peter Liba achieved distinction as a journalist, as a broadcasting executive, and as a Lieutenant Governor of Manitoba.

Peter Liba (1964)

Peter Liba – the journalist who became the Lieutenant Governor of Manitoba (1964 photo)

The Winnipeg-born Liba began his newspaper career with the *Portage la Prairie Daily Graphic* and the *Neepawa Press* before joining *The Winnipeg Tribune* in 1959. At the Trib he served in the paper's coveted Legislative Bureau for a period of time before becoming assistant city editor. When Nick Hills left the city editor post to go to Southam in 1967, Liba moved into that position.

Liba's association with the CanWest Global Group, where he was one of the founding shareholders, began in 1974, and he held various positions including president and CEO of CKND Television and SaskWest Television, as well as executive vice-president of CanWest Global Communications. He was appointed to the position of Lieutenant Governor in 1999 and served until 2004. Liba received numerous honours, including membership in the Order of Canada in 1984, and he became the first member of the Order of Manitoba in 1999.

Peter Liba died in June, 2007 at the age of 67.

NAMES IN THE FREEZER

Ann Henry had a unique way of dealing with individuals whose actions annoyed or offended her. In spite of her formidable skill with words, she would write the name of a person, along with a few relevant comments, on a small piece of paper, fold it up, and put it in the freezer section of her refrigerator. Some of her acquaintants report that, at times, the freezer held a sizeable accumulation of the chilly castigations.

Harry Mardon

To many *Tribune* readers, Harry Mardon was the paper's most forthright proponent of conservative viewpoints. Born in England in 1926 and raised in Scotland, he attended the prestigious Gordonstoun School. Mardon migrated to Canada after an impressive military career and worked with British United Press for eight years before joining *The Tribune* in 1958. He served successively as assistant city editor, city editor, editorial page editor, and business editor. He left *The Tribune* in 1966 for a public relations position with Investors Group, but then returned to the newspaper in 1969. Mardon continued with *The Tribune* as associate editor with responsibility for business news until the paper shut down in 1980.

In person as well as in his writings, Harry Mardon often came across as dogmatic and overbearing. Yet there were aspects of Mardon that softened this perception. Dona Harvey describes him as "someone who on the surface appeared to be a person of bombast, but in fact was an excellent colleague, a good digging journalist, and a person of integrity and warmth."

Harry Mardon unfalteringly positioned himself in the small "c" conservative end of *The Tribune's* polarity, and Frances Russell clearly resided in small "l" liberal territory. Yet, when Russell first joined *The Tribune*, Mardon became her mentor. "I have a very soft spot for Harry," she comments. "On every count you would think we were poles apart and would clash." When he assigned her to cover the Legislature in 1964, a time when Duff Roblin's Conservatives were in power, Mardon told her something that has stayed with her since. "The government has every imaginable kind of way to get its message across to the public. We serve to make sure that we even the playing field with the opposition."

Mardon, and his English-Scottish brogue, were often parodied – he was satirized by the University of Winnipeg's *Uniter* under the name of "Harry Hard-on" – but Jan Kamienski points out that "you could kid Harry and he wouldn't get riled."

Harry Mardon died in 2004.

Jack Matheson

When Jack Matheson returned from his stint with the Navy in 1945 and needed work, he went to *The Tribune* and asked for a job as a sports writer. The managing editor, John Gordon replied "Come in tomorrow morning and we'll put you to work."

"I don't know what they saw in me," Matheson reflects. "I didn't give them the hard sell. I was too nervous. I was very lucky – it was the best job in the world. I was a sports nut. I wanted to write sports. It's the only job I ever wanted."

Like most of his contemporaries, Matty (as he's known to legions of sports fans) has no formal training in journalism. In fact, he recalls, "I don't even know if there were journalism courses in those days." The closest he came to before-the job training was listening to Foster Hewitt hockey broadcasts on the radio and then writing the games up on his typewriter at home.

Matheson began his writing career covering university sports, then basketball, then golf, before graduating to the Blue Bomber beat, an area he covered at home and away for 27 years. He was named *The Tribune's* Sports Editor in 1959.

Following the closing of *The Tribune* in 1980, Matty was "rescued from the breadline" in 1981 by CJOB. In his radio career, he did daily sports comments and travelled with the Bombers for twelve years. In 1991, he was the author of the book *60 Years and Running*, which marked the 60th anniversary of the Winnipeg Blue Bombers.

At press time, Jack Matheson was retired and living in west Winnipeg.

In the midst of a raging debate in 1959 over the issue of allowing professional sports in Manitoba on Sundays, Hamiota United Church Rev. Ralph Clark (left) wrote a letter to the editor commenting that if he ever had to send his brains to the cleaners, he'd get a job as a sportswriter while they were gone. This understandably antagonized Jack Matheson (right), who recalls, "One thing led to another and I wound up spending a week in Hamiota and delivered a heartfelt sermon on the subject of Sunday sport." The dispute became a coast-to-coast story and made the pages of *Time* magazine.

Frank Morriss (wearing fedora, leaving in 1968 with the Winnipeg Ballet for a European trip) became *The Tribune's* entertainment columnist in the mid-60s after working for the *Free Press* for many years. Shortly after retiring, he and his wife died in a car accident while on a trip in eastern Canada.

SO HOT YOU COULDN'T FRY AN EGG

During a particularly searing heat wave in 1936, Victor V. Murray and Vince Leah ventured out into one-hundred-Fahrenheit heat to determine if the sidewalk in front of *The Tribune* Building was hot enough to fry a proverbial egg. The experiment proved that it wasn't that hot, but the pair were approached by a curious woman who had noticed the eggy mess and, assuming that someone had jumped from the building, asked where the body had been taken.

(Below) He was known as V. V. M. and Graham N. Smith (1975 photo); (Right) John Robertson earned respect as a newspaper writer, a broadcaster, and a founder of the Manitoba Marathon (1978 photo).

Victor V. Murray

At various times, Victor V. Murray wrote under his full name, under his initials 'V. V. M.', and under the pen name he adopted that not all Tribune readers realized was really a variation on the location of *The Tribune* Building – 'Graham N. Smith'. Although Murray served as *The Tribune*'s police reporter for a period of time, he became best known for his chatty columns "Tribune Trumps" (written under his own name) and "Moss I Gather" (written as Graham N. Smith).

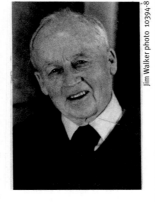

Jim Walker photo 10394-8

Like many of his journalist colleagues, the quiet, easygoing Murray was once a heavy drinker. After he decided to quit drinking, he habitually consumed copious quantities of water as he sat typing at his desk.

John Robertson

Like several of his colleagues at *The Tribune*, John Robertson followed a path that wove between the print and broadcast media. He joined *The Tribune* in 1958 as a sports writer after a couple of years at the *Regina Leader-Post*. Robertson left Winnipeg for Montreal in 1968, and during his nine years in that city worked for the *Montreal Star* and two radio stations. He returned to Winnipeg in 1977 to work with CBC television as an interviewer on *24 Hours*, and contributed a regular sports column to the *Free Press*. After an unsuccessful bid to be elected in the 1981 provincial election, Robertson was a sports columnist for various papers until 1989. He is the author of four books.

John Robertson earned the respect of his fellow newspaper journalists not only for his achievements as an outstanding sports writer, but also for a bizarre sense of humour that devised hilarious (and sometimes ribald) headlines. Robertson acquired the lasting gratitude of Manitobans when his vision of better lives for Manitobans with intellectual disabilities inspired the establishment of the Manitoba Marathon in 1979.

As this book went to press, John Robertson was living in rural Manitoba.

Frances Russell

Frances Russell had always wanted to write, but when, armed with a BA degree in history and political science, she approached the *Winnipeg Free Press* in 1962, Russell was told, "We've already got a woman in the newsroom." She found The *Tribune* more receptive, and began as a general assignment reporter, moved to the education beat, and then in 1964 became a member of the *Tribune* bureau at the Legislature.

In those days, coverage of events at the Legislature was extensive, and being a bureau member was considered a plum position for journalists. Each newspaper assigned four or five reporters to the Legislature to cover developments from morning until closing. To make final editions, stories had to be phoned in by noon. While there, Russell worked alongside such notable journalists as Roger Newman, Don Newman, Steve Melnyk, and bureau chief Jim Shilliday.

Frances Russell has a passion for political
reporting (1967 photo).

Pursuing her passion for political reporting, Russell left *The Tribune* in 1965 to join the United Press International gallery in Ottawa, and during the 1965 election had the memorable experience of travelling with John Diefenbaker and some of the best-known names in Canadian political journalism in the last "train election."

Russell returned to the Trib a year later, and was assigned to the Legislature as well as being designated the religious affairs reporter. One assignment she was given in the latter role was to interview an ecumenical minister who became her husband three years later.

In 1968, Frances Russell moved to become a reporter at the *Globe and Mail* and was subsequently sent to join their Ottawa Bureau. This assignment saw her living in the luxurious Chateau Laurier for several months at *Globe and Mail* expense on the premise that "We can't have a woman there if she's not in a safe place."

The 1970s saw Russell in a number of positions. She returned to *The Tribune* in 1971, was *Free Press* legislative reporter from 1973 to 1975, worked for the *Vancouver Sun* from 1975 to 1977, and then once again returned to *The Tribune* until its demise in 1980.

In 1981, Russell rejoined the *Winnipeg Free Press* and wrote three-a-week editorial page political columns until 1999. Her forceful and articulate viewpoints have clearly placed her in the liberal zone of political journalism and have inspired countless reactions from hard-core conservatives.

Since 1999, Frances Russell has worked as a freelance journalist and has authored three local history books. At the time this book went to press in 2008, Russell continued to write a weekly column for the *Free Press* on federal and provincial politics, and her views continued to raise the hackles of right-wing readers.

Jim Shilliday

In 1950, Jim Shilliday had a job as a bank teller, but that wasn't what he wanted. He wanted to be a writer. When he applied for a job with *The Winnipeg Tribune*, the only opening was for a copy boy, a job that paid about half of what he made as a teller. Although Shilliday was 20 years old, and most copy boys were 15 or 16, he took the job.

When he thinks back on his early days with the Trib, Jim Shilliday recalls being "kind of starry-eyed" as he first got to meet journalists like Victor V. Murray, Frank Morriss, Roy Maley, and Vince Leah. "It was like going to Hollywood and meeting stars," he remembers.

Shilliday began his journalism career as a "cub" reporter. One of his first assignments was flying over the Red River Valley, helping to

Jim Shilliday got "hooked on reporting" (1975 photo).

Gene Telpner (seated left) enjoyed writing about Winnipeg's restaurants (1971 photo)

cover the 1950 flood. His next role was police reporter, and in 1951 he watched a man hang for murder. In 1952, he joined the RCAF on a five-year commission and served with NATO, flying F-86 Sabre jet fighters in England, West Germany, and France.

Shilliday returned to *The Tribune* in 1958 and stayed until it shut down in 1980. He was a police reporter, legislature reporter and political writer, copy editor, copy chief, foreign editor, news editor, city editor, assistant managing editor, and associate editor. Looking back, he sums it up by saying, "From the time I started, I was hooked on reporting."

Shilliday recalls that, in the early 1950s, "unions were an abstraction that didn't clutter our minds." On their nights off, he and other reporters would often go to *The Tribune* and hang out. One of those nights, when the reporter on duty was out, Shilliday answered the phone and took a call from a group of Argyle School parents complaining that the building was a firetrap. He offered to tour the school the next day with the parents as long as they agreed not to notify "the other newspaper." Shilliday's story not only scooped the *Free Press*, it led to the demolition and replacement of the school building. After several dozen of the complainants stopped taking the *Free Press* and switched over to *The Tribune*, Jim Shilliday was called into the business manager's office to be given a grateful handshake and a cheque for five dollars.

Two other scoops of which he's particularly proud are the building of the Grand Rapids power dam and the story of a proposed Manitoba flag. As Shilliday puts it, "Scoops are what made reporting worthwhile, and we were always after them."

After *The Tribune* closed, Jim Shilliday served briefly as a special assistant to a provincial cabinet minister, and then was the editor of the *Winnipeg Real Estate News*. As a freelance writer, he's had a number of travel stories in the *Free Press,* and has contributed to several books and magazines. His first book, *Canada's Wheat King: The Life and Times of Seager Wheeler*, was published in 2007, and won an award as the best non-fiction book of the year. When this book went to press in 2008, Jim Shilliday was living in rural Manitoba and working on a novel about Canadian pilots during the Cold War.

Gene Telpner

During the course of his career, Gene Telpner was a columnist for the *Winnipeg Free Press*, *The Winnipeg Tribune*, and the *Winnipeg Sun*. Born in Nebraska, Telpner was a captain in the US Air Force during the Second World War and a prisoner of war for thirteen months.

His journalism career began in Omaha, but after marrying Winnipegger Fritzi Shuckett, Telpner moved to Winnipeg. He began his 14-year stay with the *Free Press* by writing a bowling column, but was soon writing his trademark entertainment news. He later moved to *The Tribune* as entertainment editor, and remained there for 13 years. When the *Winnipeg Sun* was launched, Telpner was as associate editor and daily columnist.

Gene Telpner was one of Winnipeg's most popular and visible journalists, and an avid supporter of and commentator on the local dining and entertainment scene. While he was with *The Tribune*, Telpner made frequent trips to Hollywood to interview movie stars. He had a knack for obtaining "freebies" that his colleagues envied. One of his long-remembered pieces was a tongue-in-cheek story about a bumper spaghetti crop in Italy.

Dona Harvey points out that few people were aware that the outgoing and approachable Telpner had considerable difficulty hearing, and, to help him understand, his wife often made a point of repeating what others said. Harvey describes them as "a team."

Telpner is credited with bringing a chapter of Variety Club International to Winnipeg. Gene Telpner died in Winnipeg in 2005.

Peter Warren

Peter Warren was a Tribber who made the switch from print to radio and became a local legend in the process.

Warren's newspaper career began in England, where he was born. After moving to Canada, he worked as a reporter for the *Calgary Herald* and the *Saint John Telegraph-Journal* before joining *The Winnipeg Tribune* as an editor. During his years with *The Tribune* from the mid-60s to 1971, Warren served as assistant city editor, city editor, and columnist.

Warren and Jan Kamienski were responsible for editing *Showcase*, a light weekend section covering the local scene, and their planning sessions often took place over a few beers at the St. Regis Hotel. One April 1st edition told of a new animal at the Winnipeg Zoo – an improbable cross between a giraffe and an eagle. Kamienski concocted a photo montage of the creature to accompany the article, which described the noises it made, how friendly it was, and how much it loved children. Early that Monday morning, the city parks director phoned editor Tom Green to complain that the zoo had been crowded all weekend with people looking for the unusual arrival. In another April Fools' Day prank, Warren, who did book reviews, raged about a non-existent book that was so horrifically pornographic that it didn't merit a review. *The Tribune* received a flood of phone calls from readers asking where they could buy the book.

In 1971, Warren began his broadcast career with CJOB, hosting its *Action Line* call-in show. Warren's outspoken manner, his talent for unearthing facts, and his compassion for disadvantaged people and victims of injustice earned him numerous awards, including Manitoba's Order of the Buffalo Hunt. Warren left CJOB in 1998, ostensibly to retire, but shortly after moving to British Columbia he began hosting a syndicated weekend call-in show that was broadcast across Canada until 2006.

At the time this book went to press, Peter Warren was living in British Columbia and providing investigative services to victims of crime.

Peter Warren (right) interviewing Pierre Trudeau on CJOB in 1971

Jim Haggarty photo 10625-12

Charlie MacFarlane (left) with
Eric Wells at a Canadian Press
teletype machine in 1967

74-6358-165

TAKING ON ERIC WELLS

Jan Kamienski tells of a heated conversation he overheard from his vantage point next to Eric Wells' office.
Reporter Jim Hayes, who covered city hall, wrote a story that named a number of slum landlords, some of whom
were prominent Winnipeggers. The next day, a delegation of livid landlords marched into Wells's office. In one
particularly loud exchange, Kamienski heard an angry threat to sue *The Tribune*. After a few seconds, Well's
voice broke the silence as he quietly responded, "So sue." The subdued landlords quietly filed out of the office.
Within a few days, Mayor Stephen Juba, always sensitive to publicity, arranged for the houses to be brought up to
acceptable standards at public expense. The landlords were billed for the work by the city.

STOP THE PRESSES!

Jim Shilliday tells of one of his earliest experiences with *The Tribune.* "My first recollection of Val Werier when I was a copy boy was this curly-headed guy who rushed into the newsroom and shouted something like 'Stop the presses!' or 'Hold the front page!' That was the way things were done then – if there was time they would change the front page."

Val Werier covered every beat. (1975 photo).

Eric Wells

Eric Wells was a journalists' editor, respected by his colleagues for his dedication to achieving excellence in reporting. During his two-decade career with *The Tribune,* he was telegraph editor, news editor, managing editor, and editor-in-chief.

In her essay "The Last of the Terrible Men," Heather Robertson observed that Eric Wells "was probably as good an editor as [John] Dafoe had been thirty years before but absolutely different: a news man, not a pundit….He was independent, irreverent, and intrepid. He hated bullshit more than bolshevism."

As an editor, Wells encouraged journalists to strive for ongoing improvement by critiquing their articles and providing comments and suggestions, something Frances Russell describes as "an informal journalism school." While he was capable of scathing criticism of reporters' work in global terms, he was supportive of individuals and encouraged autonomy. Looking back, a number of outstanding journalists regard Eric Wells as a mentor who helped them to refine their craft.

Beyond his reputation as a print journalist, Eric Wells achieved distinction as a broadcaster (he moved to CJOB at the same time as Peter Warren and they shared the same office space); as a historian (he was the author of *Winnipeg: Where the New West Begins*); and as a co-founder of the Western Canada Pictorial Index.

A foundation in memory of Eric Wells and his sports broadcaster brother Jack Wells presents annual awards for excellence in journalism to students at Red River College.

Val Werier

Val Werier has been described as "the conscience of the community." He's been inducted into the Order of Canada and the Order of Manitoba and has received more than twenty awards in recognition of his contributions to heritage and the environment. He's been an advocate for social justice and a champion of disadvantaged people for more than six decades. And, in his characteristically unassuming way, Val Werier simply observes "I feel proud that I've done something for Winnipeg."

Born in 1917, Val Werier grew up in Winnipeg's North End, attending William Whyte, Machray, Aberdeen, and St. John's schools. His devotion to social justice was fostered by his parents, Russian Jews who fled to Canada in 1908. His father had escaped from Siberia after attempting to organize barrel makers in Odessa.

Werier had hoped to become an architect, but his family couldn't afford to send him to university. Instead, he chose to become a journalist, beginning as a freelancer in 1938 by submitting unsolicited articles to *The Winnipeg Tribune* on topics he thought they wouldn't otherwise cover. He took on the "hotels and rails" beat at night, knowing that staff reporters were assigned to the hotels and railway stations only during the day, "to see who came to town." A polite and soft-spoken man, Werier got to know the station agents and desk clerks, and some went out of their way to tip him off about interesting people who had arrived in the city. He was paid 20 cents a column inch for articles that were published, "so I might work a whole night for seventy cents or a dollar."

In 1941, Werier was hired by city editor Fred O'Malley as a general assignment reporter. Not long after, he left *The Tribune* to become an RCAF navigator during World War Two, surviving a crash that left him with permanent back and leg injuries. "I was lucky to come back," he mentions.

Werier returned to *The Tribune* in 1945, initially to the police beat, where his counterpart from the *Free Press,* Gordon Sinclair Sr., helped him find his way around as a newcomer. After that, "I covered every beat," Werier says with quiet pride. He was a general assignment reporter, columnist, city editor, news editor, and associate editor. After *The Tribune* closed in 1980, he began contributing columns to the *Free Press* on a freelance basis.

BEER AND SKITS

The annual spectacle of Beer and Skits began in 1934, founded by *The Tribune's* Nate Zimmerman. It had a tradition of rules, including no consumption of beer by performers until after the show, no smut, no religion, and no depiction of women onstage. It had another tradition that, despite Zim's best efforts, generally trumped the first: ignoring the rules. Beer and Skits was a series of skits and sketches, parodies and lampoons, often depicting politicians and other public figures who were sitting in the audience. The performances were generally unpolished, but the drunker the performers and the audience became, the funnier and more clever the sketches appeared to be. The fare for the evening was simple – all the beer you could drink and some incidental sandwiches. Admission in the 1960s was ten bucks, and tickets were in great demand, often snapped up by politicians, lawyers, and businessmen eager to see themselves and their colleagues crudely lambasted. Until the early 1980s, women were not allowed to attend.

(1952)

The impact of Val Werier's writing in *The Tribune* is evidenced in many areas. His advocacy of environmental issues pre-dates 1950, long before the environment became a popular cause. He pioneered discussion on Dutch Elm Disease and prodded government officials to take steps to protect the trees. He raised the issues of heritage buildings before bylaws were enacted to protect them. He was largely responsible for improvements in the city's landscaping requirements for commercial sites ("I raised hell about the fact that there was no requirement for any landscaping for parking and commercial establishments in Winnipeg."). In 1968, he was the first journalist to publicize the prospect of developing The Forks which he describes as "the most dramatic stretch of property in Winnipeg."

Val Werier celebrated his 90th birthday in 2007. As this book went to press in 2008, he continued to contribute occasional columns to the *Free Press*, emphasizing the importance of protecting parks, forests, and the water quality of Lake Winnipeg.

10260-11

Nate Zimmerman

Nathan Zimmerman was the founder of *Beer and Skits* and tried his best (usually with minimal success) to enforce the rules of "good taste" during the event. He died in 1951, but some believe his ghost continued to watch over *Beer and Skits*.

"Zim," as he was affectionately called, was a drama critic and editor for *The Tribune*, but was probably best known as the host of the staff's annual Christmas party. Zimmerman was Jewish, but each year he paid out of his own pocket for the food and liquor for the event. Some Tribbers still recall with affection the sight of Zim, presiding as the bartender while standing in the slot of the news desk and wearing a Christmas hat. Folding tables were set up in the newsroom and covered in sheets of newsprint. There were generally some skits from different departments and a few speeches. There were always plenty of laughs.

COUNTING THE STARS

For many of its years, *The Tribune* published two main editions each weekday, with a line of stars printed at the top of the front page signifying the edition. The morning edition (one star), was shipped by bus at 5:00 or 6:00 a.m. to rural communities and sold by vendors on Winnipeg streets. This was actually the final edition from the previous afternoon, with a new front page and city page. The final edition was a completely new paper and was the version delivered after school by paper boys (and increasingly more paper girls) to home subscribers in the city. Depending on how news broke during the day, and particularly in the pre-television era, the front page might be re-plated more than once on a day, with a star added each time. Because the *Free Press* also had a morning edition, *Tribune* editors skimmed through their competitor's paper to check for potential stories to pursue. The *Free Press* followed the same routine with the morning *Tribune*.

Nick Hills (left) and A. Ron Williams with the MacLaren Award, a stylized lead type tray (1965)

☐ ☐ ☐ ☐ ☐ *The Tribune's* PUBLISHERS

Mark Edgar Nichols: 1920 to 1936

Wesley McCurdy: 1936 to 1948

A. W. Moscarella: 1948 to1951

F. S. Auger: 1951 to 1959

Ross Munro 1959 to 1965

A. Ron Williams: 1965 to 1977

E. H. (Bill) Wheatley: 1977 to 1980

A Legacy of Images

2

Gregg Burner, Frank Chalmers, Jim Walker, Gerry Hart

Joe McLennan photo

Trib reporter Gregg Shilliday would do anything to get on the front page, including letting Red River Ex snake handlers wrap this 200 pound python around him.

They were known as "photographers" rather than "photojournalists," and the importance of their work was often underestimated. The passage of time has helped to reveal the inherent quality and the enduring value of the work of the photographers of *The Winnipeg Tribune*.

The Tribune's Photographers

Foreword
by Gregg Shilliday

When I was a young reporter at *The Tribune* during its final days, the photographers were the cowboys of the newsroom. By that I mean they didn't have to wear ties or suits, they always got to drive the cars to assignments (invariably at high speed) and, if we were out on the town, they usually got the girls.

The Trib photographers were also fearless. If there was a fire, they figured out a way to get up closer than any sane reporter wanted to go. If some editor wanted a panorama from the top of a new high-rise, there was no shortage of volunteers. And if a cop or hospital administrator ordered no pictures, you could count on our guys to be surreptitiously shooting from the hip.

Mainly though, it was about the front page. Reporter or photographer, that was the place you wanted to be. I loved going out on assignment with photographers because their great picture might drag my story onto the front.

It goes without saying that most of the Trib shooters were also a little bit crazy. One example sticks in my memory. Jim Wiley and I were assigned to cover the evacuation of Red Lake during a huge forest fire. After the last citizen had been choppered out, we convinced the helicopter pilot to fly us over the centre of the blaze so that Jim could get a picture.

We sat on benches in the lower level of the Sikorsky with the sliding doors open so that Jim would have an unobstructed view. As we hovered over the fiery inferno, Jim pulled on the headphones and shouted something to the pilot. The chopper suddenly flipped on its side. Having no warning as to what Jim had asked for, I went hurtling down the bench towards the open door. At the

last second, I grabbed a piece of webbing and hauled myself to my seat.

Later, back on terra firma, I yelled a bit and told Jim I had just missed falling into the centre of a raging forest fire.

Jim shook his head sadly. "Really? Boy, that would have made for a hell of a picture."

Media people posed on a luggage hoist at the Winnipeg Airport in May, 1974 during a royal visit. Trib photographers: Gregg Burner (seated with arms outstretched) and Gerry Cairns (standing at right, wearing checked sports coat). The others are unidentified CBC personnel.

Photo courtesy Jeff De Booy

□ □ □ □ □

(Right) Gordon Aikman and Val Werier covering the 1950 flood.

Gordon Aikman

Gordon Aikman was born in Dauphin in 1914, dropping out of school in grade eight to help support his family. He did freelance news photography for *The Winnipeg Tribune* while working for a photo studio in Dauphin. His subsequent move to Winnipeg led not only to his hiring by the Trib as a staff photographer, but also to his meeting news reporter Alice McEachern and to their 57-year marriage. Aikman's 40-year career with *The Tribune* was interrupted for his service in World War II, where he was a military photographer and took photos in the front-line heat of battle. He and his crew were among the first Canadians to re-enter Dieppe after it was liberated, and their photos are in the Canadian War Archives.

After returning to *The Tribune*, Aikman became the photo editor, a position he held until his retirement in 1979, and he served as a mentor for a series of photographers, most notably Frank Chalmers. The subjects of Aikman's photos included a number of Canadian prime ministers,

(Left) Gordon Aikman (shown with his wife Alice) took a leave of absence from *The Tribune* in 1942 to enlist with the army as a private. He was sent overseas in 1944 as a photographer with the rank of lieutenant. While in Holland, Aikman became ill and was sent home on a stretcher.

such celebrities as Jack Dempsey, Fats Waller, Louis Armstrong, and the legendary photographer Yousuf Karsh, who described Aikman as "a fine photographer who tells the truth." Some of Gordon Aikman's most impressive legacies are a series of black and white portraits of Manitoba churches he took in the late 1970s.

Columnist Frances Russell remembers Gordon Aikman as "the absolute consummate gentleman and a professional right down to the soles of his shoes." Editor Dona Harvey remarks that, when she was in the editor's office, "He was the quiet person that I would sometimes go to for advice. I'd shut the door and say 'Gordon, I have a problem.'" Sports editor Jack Matheson describes him as "the consummate pro." Gordon Aikman died in 2002.

Photo courtesy Katie Chalmers-Brooks

THE SINKINGS OF THE ANDREA DORIA

Gerry Haslam passes on the story of photo editor Gordon Aikman's ongoing campaign to convince editor Tom Green to obtain a wirephoto machine. When the Andrea Doria sank in 1956, the Free Press obtained by wire a photo of the ship keeling over and sinking, but the Trib, which relied on mail and courier service, was able to obtain such photos only a day or two after they were taken. The story goes that Aikman stormed into Green's office holding up copies of the Free Press and *The Tribune* side by side, the Free Press featuring a prominent photo and an extensive news story, *The Tribune* containing only the headline story. "Tom, I've been saying for months that we should have a wire photo machine, and now the Free Press has the Andrea Doria sinking and we don't," the frustrated Aikman complained. Green sat back in his chair, thought for a few moments, and countered, "Ah, but Gordon, how many times will the Andrea Doria sink?"

Gordon Aikman photo

This shot of a young baseball player arguing with an umpire was one of Gordon Aikman's personal favourites. Taken on May 24, 1952, it won the Canadian Press Photo of the Month award. The argumentative 8-year-old was Leo Duguay, who represented St. Boniface in the House of Commons from 1984 to 1988.

Yousuf Karsh was one of many famous individuals to become the subjects of portraits by Gordon Aikman

Gordon Aikman photo

Gordon Aikman photo Photo Courtesy Katie Chalmers-Brooks

A torrential rain in 1939 (the heaviest since 1914) sent
Portage Avenue pedestrians scurrying for shelter

MEETING GORDON AIKMAN: JEFF DE BOOY

"The first time I walked into *The Tribune* newsroom and I saw Gord Aikman sitting behind
a desk, he was the epitome of the fifties press man. I could envision him wearing a
fedora with a "Press" card. He had a thin moustache and slicked-back hair. His image
was like walking back to the fifties."

Photo courtesy Katie Chalmers-Brooks

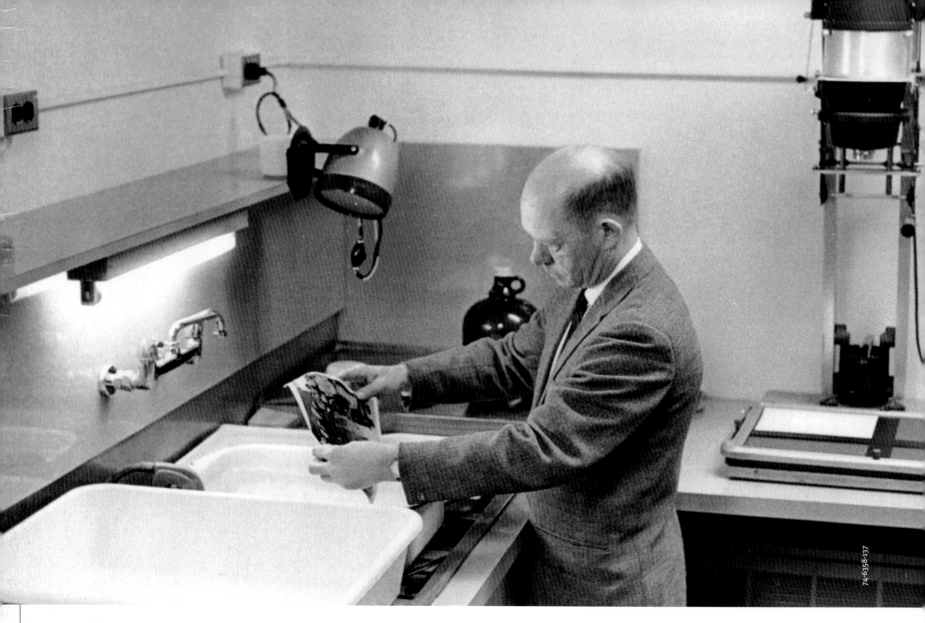

(Above) Hugh Allan in the newly-renovated *Tribune* photographic department (1967).

(Opposite) This October, 1952 photo of the Manitoba Legislature was taken by Hugh Allan after the first snowfall of the season at about 9:00 in the evening. He shot it as a time exposure and lit the foreground by driving his car back and forth with the headlights on.

Hugh Allan

Hugh Allan began with *The Tribune* as a freelance photographer during the 1950 Red River flood. This led to a full-time position as a staff photographer and eventually to his becoming the newspaper's chief photographer.

During his career with the Trib, Allan covered news and sporting events, including the Winnipeg Blue Bombers, the Winnipeg Jets, and the Canada-Russia hockey series. He was named to the media rolls of honour of both the Manitoba Sportswriters and Sportscasters Association and the Winnipeg Blue Bombers.

His daughter Janice recalls that Allan was once given an award for his aerial photography, a hard-earned merit because he suffered from motion sickness and always flew with a doggy bag.

An innovative photographer, Allan was a pioneer in the use of "bounce lighting," a technique he utilized to soften harsh shadows created by a flash, particularly when shooting people on location. He was also one of the first photographers to shoot panoramic views before wide-angle lenses were available. He took three or four different views of a scene by changing the camera angle and then printed, mounted and framed them as one photograph.

Sports writer Ed Dearden recalls Hugh Allan's determination to get just the right shot. "He would do anything to get a picture – climb trees, stand on the roof of a building. At football games, he'd stand on the top of the grandstand." Jack Matheson comments, "The best photographer we ever had for sports was Hughie Allan. He always came up with a great sports picture."

Allan was an athlete in his own right and a competitor in many sports. As a young man, he ran track and played hockey. He curled and golfed his entire adult life, achieving a hole-in-one at the age of 85. His sports experience gave him exceptional anticipatory skills as a sports photographer. Allan left *The Tribune* after 25 years and started his own business. He died in 2004 at the age of 87.

(Bottom, Right) Gregg Burner was recruited by Gordon Aikman to become a photographer (1980 photo).

(Below) Gregg Burner found his niche in fashion photography.

Gregg Burner

When photo editor Gordon Aikman decided to offer copy boy Gregg Burner an opportunity to become a staff photographer in the late 1960s, he gave Burner an unusual reason: "You're young, you're bright, you know absolutely nothing about photography and you'll be a blank canvas. I can put on what I want. I don't have to unteach anything."

Burner says he accepted the offer "against my better judgement," recalling that he cautioned Aikman, "I was the least technical person I had ever met and I would likely break his equipment."

Looking back, Burner observes that Gordon Aikman "basically changed my life." As a young photographer learning his craft on the job, he was given the task of developing photos that came to *The Tribune* by wire. "I saw some of the best pictures in the world coming up, not knowing really what they were. So it was pretty hard not to be exposed to really fine photography."

Burner's assignments for the Trib covered the gamut of news topics, but he found his niche in fashion and became an outstanding fashion photographer. He left *The Tribune* just three months before the paper stopped publishing, and later moved into his present role as a financial advisor.

Gregg Burner photo 10327-4

Gregg Burner (1980)

Gregg Burner photo 10470-8

"To get this effect, you print everything else darker than the face. Sometimes I would give Gord Aikman three or four alternative prints. For the downward angle, you jump on anything you can. I used to have a box. It was steel reinforced and it was a bugger to carry around, but it would make me two feet taller than anybody else."

Photo courtesy Katie Chalmers-Brooks

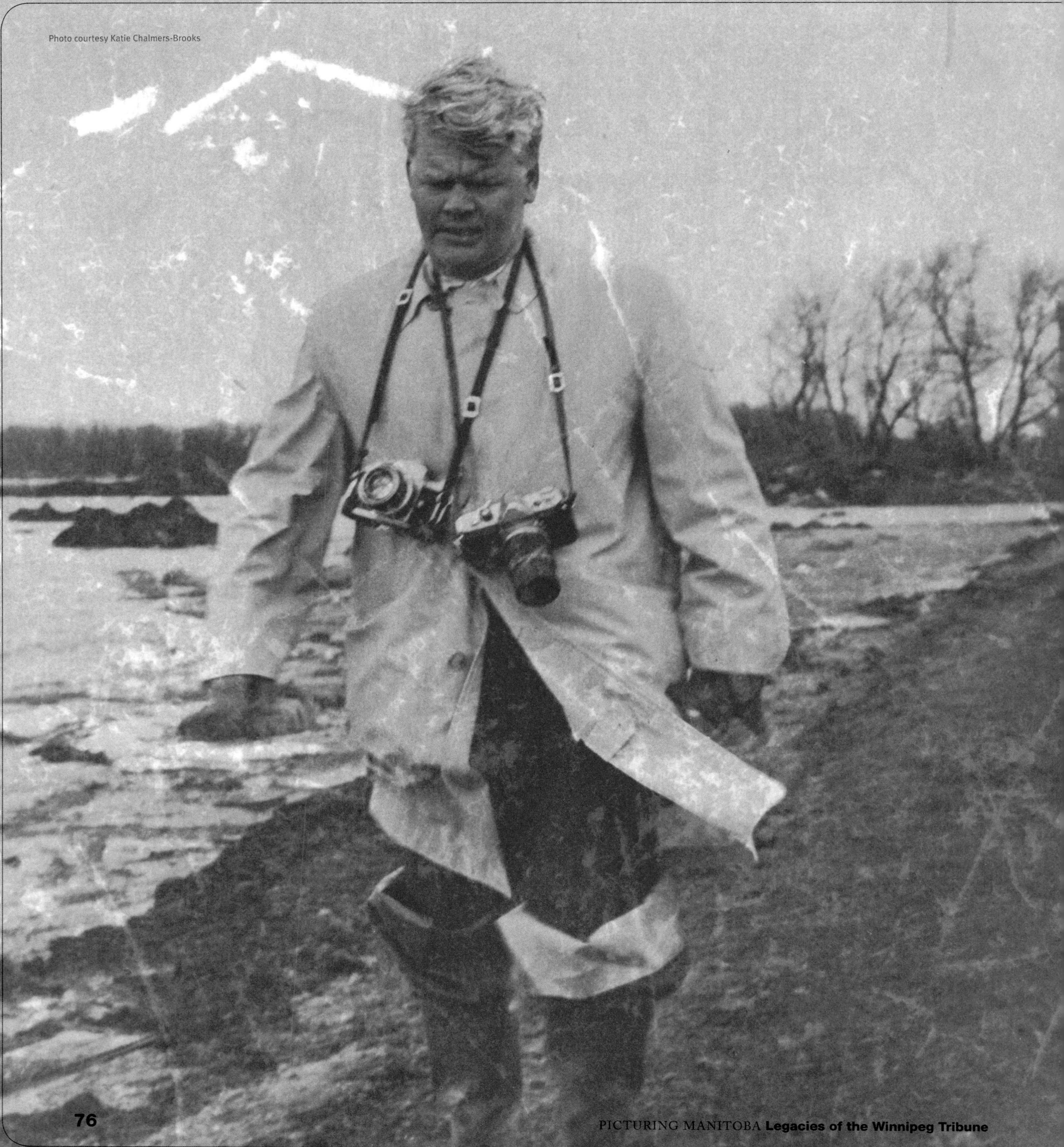

(Opposite): Frank Chalmers usually had a couple of cameras around his neck while on assignment. He liked to have spare bodies and lenses on hand and ready (Above): Frank Chalmers (wearing light-coloured suit at far right) was one of only four Canadian photographers invited to London in 1970 for a special 20-minute photo session with the Royal Family.

Frank Chalmers

Frank Chalmers grew up in Winnipeg Beach and began his career as a staff photographer with *The Tribune* in the late 1960s. He later succeeded his mentor and close friend, Gordon Aikman, as Photo Editor. His subjects ranged from Queen Elizabeth and her family at Windsor Castle, to a distraught Winnipeg woman evicted from her home. His work was seen in newspapers and magazines across the world, including *Time* magazine, the *Los Angeles Times*, the *New York Times*, *Paris Match*, and *Der Spiegel*. After the demise of *The Tribune*, Chalmers was a founding editor of the *Winnipeg Sun*.

Chalmers is praised by his fellow Trib photographer Gerry Hart as "the best that ever came out of Winnipeg, and probably one of the best in Canada." Jeff De Booy, who began his career with *The Tribune*

and is now a *Free Press* photographer, remembers with admiration Chalmers' technique in the darkroom, "His hands danced over the prints and absolutely perfect photographs came out of the processor. The range of greyscale was all there. It was a marvel to see him work." Jon Thordarson, now photo editor of the *Free Press*, describes Frank Chalmers as his mentor at *The Tribune* and points out "When he took a photograph, he knew exactly what the light was going to be. That was the key back then. It's all digital now." From a reporter's perspective, Ed Dearden remembers Chalmers as a perfectionist who would sometimes take twenty shots of something as routine as the presentation of a sports award, shooting until he got it just right. Frank Chalmers died in 2006 at the age of 62.

Opposite: One of the most powerful images ever published by *The Winnipeg Tribune* is Frank Chalmers' poignant photograph of a woman who had been evicted from her home. Chalmers used a Rolleiflex with Tri-X film, exposing at 1/250th second and f:8.

Award-Winner

On one level, this heart-wrenching photograph conveys its own story more effectively than words can express. On another level, it stimulates the need to know more about the weeping woman and the situation it portrays.

The woman's name was Lena Birch and she was 57 years old in 1967. She and her husband Frank owned a 30-acre farm north of the Perimeter Highway near McPhillips, a place where they had lived since the 1930s. The City of Winnipeg, wanting the Birch acreage and two adjacent properties for a sewage lagoon, refused their request to move their house to a nearby vacant piece of land. The Birches turned down the City's initial offer of $8,000 for the property as well as a later offer of $13,000.

Tribune staffers were aware of the family's plight and had even tipped them off that a bailiff would be arriving with an eviction notice. Frank Chalmers was there when three bailiffs and a Mountie arrived, preceded by a bulldozer. An axe was used on the locked front door, a "No Trespassing" sign was posted, and the Birches' furniture was thrown into a ditch.

Eventually Frank and Lena Birch, with the help of their son, were able to purchase a home on Burrows Avenue. The $13,000 that the City had placed in a trust account for them was left untouched until after Frank died in 1978. Lena Birch died in 1997 at the age of 87.

The photo of the distraught woman, wearing her overcoat and bedroom slippers as she virtually hugged her house for the last time, was listed by Canadian Press as one of the best 100 photos of the 20th century and was the Canadian News Photo of the Year. It appeared in newspapers across North America and was described by Robert Kennedy as "stark testimony to a system of remote and impersonal government."

(Above) "I shot it with a 28 mm wide angle, and of course back then [1976] I didn't have a motor drive, so I had to shoot it very quickly with a lot of wrist action and get out of the way. I thought a low angle would make it a more dynamic and powerful shot."

(Opposite) I had an idea for Remembrance Day [1978], and I think it ran front page. I took a picture of a wreath and a night-time photo of the Unknown Soldier at the Legislature. I used a "dodging tool" made from a coat hanger wrapped in tape and bent into a circle to hold back or "dodge" the centre area of the wreath that I didn't want printed. Then I did the reverse, using a piece of cardboard with a hole in the centre to print the photo of the Legislative Building with the Unknown Soldier. Through about 35 to 45 minutes of trial and error I managed to line them both up."

Jeff De Booy

It might have been a lack of bus fare that led to Jeff De Booy's career as a photojournalist. In 1971, De Booy had just graduated in photography and commercial arts from Tec-Voc High School and was looking for a job. One day he'd applied at the Bay for something in display or advertising and, having no bus fare, needed to walk home. On the way, he impulsively decided to drop into *The Tribune* to see if they might have an opening. De Booy was sent to managing editor Dick Goodwin,

who was so impressed with the young man's portfolio that he introduced him to photo editor Gordon Aikman. Less than a month later, De Booy received a phone call from Tom Green, who asked, "How would you like to work for *The Tribune*?" Jeff De Booy stayed at *The Tribune* until the paper closed in 1980, and was hired by the *Free Press* as a staff photographer a few years later.

Jeff De Booy

TO THE IMMORTAL MEMORY OF
THE MEN AND WOMEN FROM
ONTARIO WHO GAVE THEIR LIVES
IN THE GREAT WAR 1914-1918

LEST WE FORGET

Jeff De Booy photo 58-4837-20

JEFF DE BOOY:
"My first proud moment was when I was asked to illustrate the Royal Winnipeg Ballet's upcoming season. My idea was to photograph dancer Craig Sterling leaping in the air at Portage and Main with the Richardson Building in the background. The image in my head is that I wanted the dancer to be suspended and framed by the Richardson Building. And it actually worked. I remember the day. I was lying on the ground and it was cold. I'm sure the dancer was not very comfortable, because he was in tights and a military kind of top and I'm sure he was cold too. I asked him many times to do leaps, maybe dozens of times before I actually captured him exactly where I wanted him. It didn't seem to take very long, but it was probably a good half hour before we were done. That ran front page, quite large, and I was very proud of that."

Photo courtesy Katie Chalmers-Brooks

(Right) A 1973 Gerry Hart photo showed the pride of Boer War veterans Charles Wedley (age 91) Davey Shores (age 94).

(Above) Gerry Hart

Gerry Hart photo 68-5976-1

Gerry Hart

Like many other Tribbers, Gerry Hart began his career as a copy boy – but not at *The Tribune*. His first jobs were with the *Winnipeg Free Press*, at first as a copy boy, and later as a photo engraver on the overnight shift. Hart moved to *The Tribune* in 1970, remaining there for six years. During his time with the Trib, much of Hart's photography covered hockey, including Team Canada in 1972 and the Winnipeg Jets, and he covered general news as well.

One of his most memorable photos was the now-classic image of Bobby Hull signing his million-dollar contract at Portage and Main. Another was a waist-up shot of John Diefenbaker. Hart was given exactly one minute with Diefenbaker – enough time for only two shots.

For several decades, Gerry Hart's name has been familiar to patrons of Assiniboia Downs as the track photographer who takes the official photos of winning horses and their owners after each race. He began the part-time job in the early 1960s, continued in the role while he worked for *The Tribune*, and is still there more than forty years later.

Jon Thordarson photo 63-5605-81

"This was a few hours after the Aubigny tornado in 1978. The statue
had been up on the roof and it was now lying on the ground. I helped the
minister right the statue and took the picture. Afterwards, people were
describing it as a miracle that the statue was standing."

(Right) Jon Thordarson captured the joy of winning the AVCO Cup in 1976.

(Below) "Henry Kalen worked with my father, who was also an architect. When I was a teenager, I got to meet Henry a few times. I went to his studio with photographs and he would give me advice. He was a craftsman. He was also a terrific inventor – he'd invent things to use in his darkroom. That's his architectural camera in the photo." (1977 photo)

10616-3

Jon Thordarson (1979)

Jon Thordarson

After starting at *The Tribune* as a copy boy in 1973 Jon Thordarson was offered a job as a photographer by Frank Chalmers following the departure of Gerry Hart. Thordarson remained with the Trib until its closing in 1980, serving as the paper's chief photographer. Much of his photography was in sports, with an emphasis on the Winnipeg Jets and the Winnipeg Blue Bombers.

After *The Tribune* folded, Thordarson spent some time at the *Hamilton Spectator* and the *Winnipeg Sun* before joining the staff of the *Winnipeg Free Press* in 1989. He's currently the photo editor at the *Free Press*.

(Left) A classic Graflex Speed Graphic presented to Gordon Aikman by his *Tribune* colleagues when he retired. A plaque on the top is inscribed "To Gordon Aikman, whose skill with a camera inspired us for 40 years, 1939-1979, From all his friends at the Winnipeg Tribune"

(Below) A Nikon F2 used by Frank Chalmers. Each photographer had a favourite make of camera.

Photos courtesy Katie Chalmers-Brooks

The Cameras

From the 1930s until the late 1950s, cameras like the Graflex Speed Graphic were standard equipment in press photography. Taking photos with the heavy and bulky Speed Graphic was a slow process. It utilized 4" x 5" negatives that held only two exposures. After one shot, the slide had to be pulled out and turned around before the second photo could be taken. The Speed Graphic had no automated features; each shot required manual settings by the photographer. All indoor and most outdoor shots needed supplemental light from camera's single-use bulbs. The Graflex was most effective at a distance of only seven to ten feet from the subject, and static poses were preferable to moving subjects. These factors, in addition to the formidable appearance of the camera itself, virtually ruled out surreptitious or spontaneous photography. The classic cameras were capable of producing very high quality images when used by skilled photographers under the right circumstances.

The advent of smaller, faster, and more agile cameras in the 1960s and 1970s brought about dramatic changes in the kinds of photos that appeared in newspapers. Twin-lens reflex cameras (2 ¼" negatives and 8 to 12 exposures per roll) and subsequent 35 mm cameras (36 exposures per roll) enabled photojournalists to capture more images more quickly, to use available light, and to capitalize on the advantages of telephoto lenses. These breakthroughs enabled newspapers to provide their readers with dramatic and revealing shots of news as it happened.

The Tribune's photographers used their own cameras and equipment on the job, receiving a monthly allowance in return. This arrangement meant that *The Tribune* didn't have to purchase photographic equipment, and that the photographers were able to use the makes and models they preferred.

The photographers did their own developing in the fourth floor darkroom. Because most preferred to be alone as they processed their films, they took turns using the room.

The Assignments

At *The Tribune*, staff photographers were given assignments by the photo editor and were generally paired up with reporters. When things were busy, especially on weekends, they might have as many as fifteen assignments in a day in various parts of the city. When things were quiet, Trib photographers were encouraged to go out "enterprising" – seeking photo opportunities. The use of two-way radios began in the 1970s.

Although the relationship between reporters and photographers were generally positive, there was sometimes differing perceptions of who was in charge during an assignment. Reporters generally believed they were in the lead role, but some learned that introducing a colleague as "my photographer" wasn't appreciated. On the other hand, the photographers were the ones who did the driving and received a mileage allowance for using their cars. As Gregg Burner sees it, "A lot of reporters really thought they were in charge sometimes, but hey, we were driving."

Jim Wiley (left) and Gregg Burner in *The Tribune* darkroom (February, 1976)

Photo courtesy Jeff De Booy

Quality

Just as the rivalry between *The Tribune* and the *Free Press* motivated the journalists of each newspaper to try to outdo the other, the photographers of the two papers were constantly striving to take better photos than their competitors.

Gregg Burner says it was a "delight" to discover that one of his photos had no counterpart in the *Free Press*. He proudly recalls that

Free Press photographer Gerry Cairns once told him, "You always made me work harder."

Jeff De Booy recalls, "Every morning *The Tribune* photo department grabbed both papers and we analyzed the photographs we took compared to the photographs the *Free Press* photographers took. It was a very healthy atmosphere because it pushed us all to try to do better."

Gerry Hart is convinced that photography was more important to *The Tribune* than it was to the *Free Press* and insists that it was very seldom that the *Free Press* outdid *The Tribune* in photos. "We were picture-conscious. We devoted space to photographs and we played them the way they should be played. If a photo was suited to run as an eight-column picture, they'd run it as an eight-column picture – the full page."

Jon Thordarson recalls, "They always made room for good photography. They played up local photographs big. We'd get picture pages just at the drop of a hat. If you went out on an assignment and could generate three, four, five pictures, they'd get in the paper."

WORKING FOR *The Tribune*: GREGG BURNER

"I'd have worked at *The Tribune* for nothing. And in those days actually you could work there for peanuts because a lot of the press conferences had booze and food. A lot of the people could really drink and hold their alcohol, so they'd go and have five or six shots and a boat load of shrimp or some perogies or whatever was there, then go back and process their film or write their story."

Picturing Manitoba 3

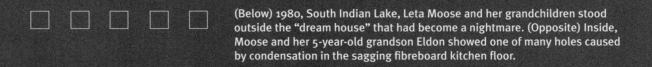

(Below) 1980, South Indian Lake, Leta Moose and her grandchildren stood outside the "dream house" that had become a nightmare. (Opposite) Inside, Moose and her 5-year-old grandson Eldon showed one of many holes caused by condensation in the sagging fibreboard kitchen floor.

ABORIGINAL LIFE

Peter Levick photo 50-3559-5

Peter Levick photo 50-3559-4

Frank Chalmers photo 46-2983-36

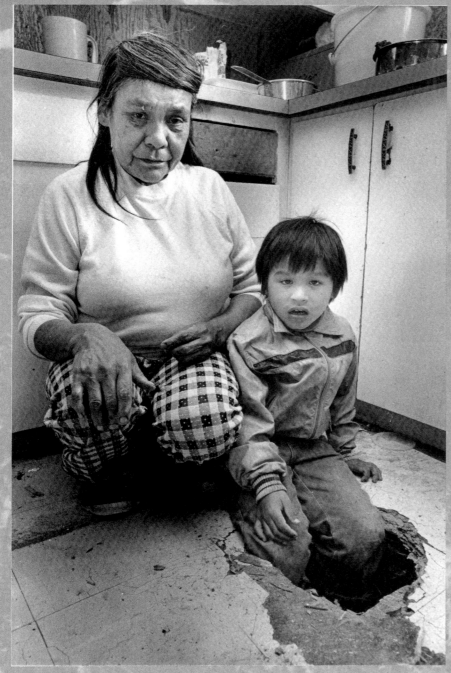

(Above) John Wheeler, a 70-year-old Brokenhead Reserve resident and a special forces veteran of World War Two and Korea, wore his medals with pride (1975).

44-2740-12

A Love-In at Assiniboine
Park (1967)

44-2740-4

THE AGE OF THE HIPPIE

Frank Chalmers photo courtesy of Katie Chalmers-Brooks

One of Frank Chalmers' most reproduced photos, this novelty shot appeared in newspapers around the world.

A Roseberry Street resident complained about her neighbour's birdhouses (1976).

□ □ □ □ □

(Left)) Like the chicken soup photo, this shot by Frank Chalmers was used by numerous newspapers. The dog's right paw is strapped to the pedal.

Frank Chalmers photo courtesy of Katie Chalmers-Brooks

Ron Dobson photo 25-699-29

Gerard Kwiatkowski photo 45-2784-44

(Left)) Reminiscent of the Alfred Hitchcock movie, *The Birds*, a 1979 gathering of swallows near Morley Avenue undoubtedly made some residents uneasy.

(Above) Rider Carla Wall and her horse High Bluff came to a sudden stop at the Winnipeg Horsemen's Club 34th annual horse show at Bird's Hill Park in May, 1980.

THE AUDITORIUM AND THE ARENA

(Above) The Winnipeg
Auditorium (1965)

(Opposite) A huge portrait
of the Queen watched over
all Arena events, including
Winnipeg Jets games
(1978 photo).

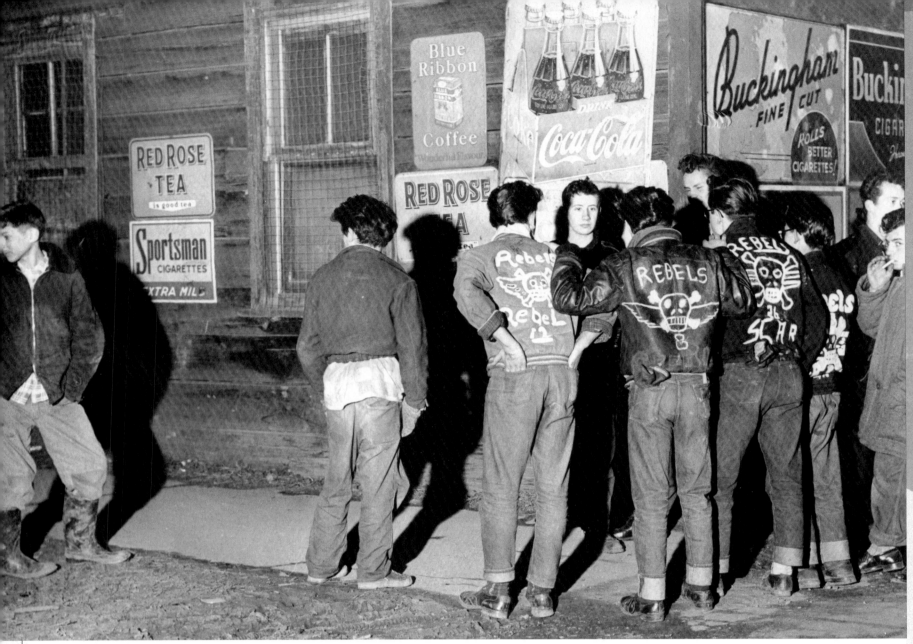

31-1348-27

(Above) Winnipeg teen gang members posed for a *Tribune* photographer in 1957.

(Right) Published caption (November 3, 1977): "TV video games – electronic devices that make the television set an arcade game"

☐ BEING A TEENAGER

Jon Thordarson photo

65-5538-33

Jim Walker photo 56-4506-3

(Top) A pinball tournament (1979)

(Bottom) Paul Brigden and five friends held a skateboarding fundraiser to break a Guinness World Record in 1979.

Jim Walker photo 63-5263-3

□ BINGO NIGHT

30-1178-69

(Above) Tuesday night bingo at the Norberry Community Club (1967);
(Opposite) William Kardash calling bingo numbers at the Ukrainian
Labour Temple (1978)

□ □ □ □ □

Boy Scouts and Venturers from around the world during the
closing ceremonies of the Manitoba Jamboree at Bird's Hill
Park in July, 1980

BOY SCOUTS THROUGH THE YEARS

(Above) Boy Scouts in 1958

(Left) First Assiniboia Boy Scout Troop, April, 1915

Frank Chalmers photo 72-6267-20

(Left) Transit driver Paul Dion greeted passengers with a smile in 1969.

(Below) Winnipeg Electric Streetcars on Portage Avenue near Newton Street (ca. 1950) Streetcars were discontinued in Winnipeg in 1955.

(Opposite) Overhead heated outlets outside the Winnipeg Central Gas Building on Notre Dame used "cosmic rays" to keep Winnipeggers warm while waiting for the bus in February, 1962.

BUSES AND STREETCARS

72-6267-81

Three 1967 photos by Frank Chalmers portrayed Winnipeg's Chinatown.

PICTURING MANITOBA

21-223-1

59-4915-90

□ CHURCHES

BEHIND THE CAMERA

During the late 1970s, Gordon Aikman and his wife Alice enjoyed drives through Manitoba, and along the way he took photographs of churches. The photos, like the buildings they presented, were unpretentious.

(Left) St. Anne's Anglican Church near Poplar Point, Manitoba was completed in 1864 and was one of the oldest log churches in continuous use in western Canada (June, 1978).

(Right) Roman Catholic Church Notre Dame de Lourdes Manitoba (published December 24, 1978)

Myrtle United Church, Myrtle Manitoba (published November 4, 1978)

66-5710-1

(Above) Published caption (December 31, 1977): "St. Vladimir and Olga Ukrainian Greek Orthodox Church Gilbert Plains Manitoba" (Opposite) Published caption (August 26, 1978): "Ukrainian Greek Catholic Church Cooks Creek Manitoba. The Church was built between 1930 and 1952 entirely by volunteer labour under the direction of the Very Reverend Father Phillip Ruh, who also built churches in a similar style at Dauphin and Neepawa."

COVERING A HANGING

(Right) The view from the Headingley Gaol (Jail) "Death Cell," just a few steps from the gallows.

BEHIND THE CAMERA

It took place almost six decades ago, but Jim Shilliday vividly remembers the hanging he covered at Headingley Gaol. In 1951 Shilliday was a young police reporter for *The Tribune*, eager to be a writer and to do a good job for the newspaper. He was assigned to cover a hanging and that was what he did.

Shilliday and his *Free Press* counterpart were far from alone in witnessing the event. There were around thirty official observers, including six or eight people from the coroner's jury, some sheriffs, and some Winnipeg Police Department and RCMP officers. The convicted murderer whose last moments they gathered to watch had drunkenly stabbed a mother of six eighteen times with an ice pick in a sleazy Main Street hotel room, then stuffed her body under the bed.

When the time came, Shilliday and the other witnesses were ushered through a cell block that had been emptied of its occupants to an area surrounding a raised platform bordered by a wooden railing. He remembers looking up at the platform and seeing a rope attached in readiness to a wooden beam, and a giant lever that looked like a railway switch. Three wooden steps – not the storied thirteen – led from the floor to the platform.

Just before 1:00 a.m., two burly guards, one on each side, half-escorted, half-carried the condemned man, probably drugged to numb his awareness, his feet barely touching the floor, his eyes darting upward and around. It all happened very quickly. "He was out of the door, to the steps, up the steps, a black hood was pulled over his head," Shilliday recounts. The hangman, "a bald, stoutish man with an overstuffed squeaky face who looked like a wrestler who'd been in too many fights" quickly put the noose over the man's head and bellowed, "Stand back!" The guards retreated, and the hangman yanked the lever that opened the trap doors on which the man stood.

Shilliday remembers that the moment the man dropped into the pit below the platform, the observers scrambled onto the platform to stare down at him. Few bothered to use the steps. Most swung over the railing and crowded around the opening to peer into the pit. Shilliday, being a reporter, remembers scanning their faces, fascinated by their expressions.

The coroner gingerly descended a steep staircase into the pit, undid the top buttons of the man's shirt, and listened with his stethoscope for a heartbeat. He did that three times. On the third examination, he finally gave a signal that the man was dead.

The body was carried from the pit and laid out, its face beet red, its tongue protruding grotesquely. The coroner discreetly tucked the tongue back into its mouth.

A reception followed in the nearby kitchen. There were sandwiches, coffee, cakes, and jelly roll. The hangman, in a heavy French-Canadian accent, complimented himself on having gotten the weight and the drop just right. Jim Shilliday was so focussed on reporting the story accurately that he didn't react as a person to what he had just witnessed. That came later.

62-5135-3

THE DAYS OF ONE-ROOM SCHOOLS

62-5135-2

62-5135-4

Glimpses of a
one-room school (1949).

36-2258-9

BASKERVILLE SCHOOL.

PRIVATE
NO
TRESPASSING

Abandoned Baskerville School
(1965)

(Opposite) Published caption
(February 23, 1980): "Teacher
Lorna Wiebe rings the bell to call
students to class in the Birkenhead
school at Neuenburg, near Winkler.
Birkenhead is one of the few one-
room schools still in use in the
province; eighteen children take
classes there. Parents in the area
decided they would keep the school
rather than have their children
bused to a more modern one."

☐ THE COMPUTER ERA

Jeff De Booy photo 10031-9

Gregg Burner photo 30-1196-21

(Clockwise)
Published caption (January 13 1978): "Winnipeg has entered the era of small affordable computers which have turned sci-fi into kitchen counter reality and raised the possibility of a computer in every home"

Published caption (October 4, 1979): "Ted Nelson holds a hand computer that has been developed for use in the home"

Published caption (January 13, 1979): "Dr. William Blight sees computer as a way to cut down on time-consuming paperwork"

☐ ☐ ☐ ☐ ☐

Jeff De Booy photo 30-1196-55

Jim Walker photo 33-1974-14

DISCO DAZE

(Above) Published caption (May 31, 1979): "Winnipeg's newest disco, Studio 44, will be "one of the best (disco) places in Canada," according to president Jimmy Ginakes. The dance floor is glass, covering neon stars - a flashy place for disco fans to show off their latest steps. Winnipeg now sports nine disco spots."

(Right) J's Discotheque opened at 244 Smith Street (previously the home of the Aragon Ballroom and the Rainbow Dance Gardens) in 1965. The opening bands were the Jury, the Shondells, and the In-Crowd, with radio deejay Daryl Burlingham (known as "Daryl B") as emcee.

33-1734-1

(Above) Volcanic ash from the 1980 eruption of Mount St. Helens in the state of Washington reached Winnipeg, and Paulette George and daughter Genevieve wore dust masks as they crossed the Lagimodiere overpass near Nairn.

(Left) Lily Schreyer test drove an electric car (1975).

☐ ENVIRONMENTAL ISSUES

Jeff De Booy photo 10600-1

24-493-24

(Above) Dr. David Suzuki chatting with students (1972)

(Left) Pearl McGonigal recharging an electric car (1970)

Frank Chalmers photo 59-4890-20

(Above) Frank Chalmers set up a shot of an exceptionally accommodating "Orbit" highway trash receptacle in 1969.

(Opposite) Demonstration of mosquito fogging on Smith Street near the *Tribune* Building in 1949.

Jeff De Booy photo 69-6184-42

AN ERA OF PROTEST

Published caption (August 31, 1979): "Anti-Apartheid Movement members picketed the liquor store at Portage Avenue and Victor Street Thursday to protest the sale of South African liquor in Manitoba"

Jeff De Booy photo 50A-3675-1

Published caption (March 5, 1979): "Manitoba Peace Council marchers carried pickets calling for China to pull back from Vietnam"

Pro-Choice march (1970)

20-13-1

"Rick the Freak" during the hippie era (1969)

10060-13

Gregg Burner photo 10006-12

□ FACES OF MANITOBANS

(Above) Published caption (July 18, 1979): "Gottfried Ammeter, 84, patriarch of the family, is surrounded by some of the 230 clan members gathered in Starbuck Saturday"

(Right) Typical "Society Page" photo, published May 5, 1951

10046-3

Jim Walker photo 29-1614-32

27-1341-23

Frank Chalmers photo 37-2307-28

(Clockwise)
A tobacco blending bar (1977)

Winnipeg firefighter
(March, 1975)

"Oldest Legionnaire" Bill Caswell
(age 89) and Cadet Paul Riedle
(age 13) in 1976

Jeff De Booy photo 61-5068-16

BEHIND THE CAMERA

JEFF DE BOOY: "I was trying for a serious picture, but Father Abbott was very jovial. The composition was very important to me, the arches in the back. With most of my portraits, I usually have preconceived ideas of what they should look like. This was one of my first feature assignments. It was part of a series on Trappist Monks."

Photographer's note (May 26, 1973): "(left to right) Brother Nestor, Father Lucien, Father Abbot reading from a 'psalter' (Book of Psalms) in the Abbaye Notre-Dame-des-Prairies"

(Opposite) Brian Rhon (14) and Jackie Chetyrbok (16) with other members of the Zirka Dance Ensemble in a dress rehearsal for the Dauphin Ukrainian Festival (1980)

Jim Wiley photo 52-4000-29

☐ THE FESTIVALS OF SUMMER

(Above) Morden Corn and Apple Festival (1975)

(Right) Gimli Icelandic Festival (1974)

☐ ☐ ☐ ☐ ☐

Frank Chalmers photo 46-2879-23

(Above) Boissevain Turtle Derby
(1975)

(Left) Steinbach Pioneer Days
(1975)

Morris Stampede (1975)

MANITOBA MARATHON FINI

Jim Walker photo 50-3662-22

Jim Wiley photo 50-3662-16

(Top) Helping hands; (Bottom) The finish line for the first marathon was inside the Winnipeg Stadium.

Jim Wiley photo 50-3662-14

28-1512-1

(Above) Delivering Champ's Kentucky Fried Chicken (1964)

(Left) The Bridge Drive-In (popularly known as "The BDI") in 1979

Joe McLellan photo 26-809-1

☐ THE FLAVOURS OF WINNIPEG

(Above) Blake Morden with a customer at Morden's Candies (1976)

(Far Left) Decorating a chocolate Easter Bunny at Cavalier Candies (1980)

(Left) Stuffing bologna at Winnipeg Old Country Sausage (1978)

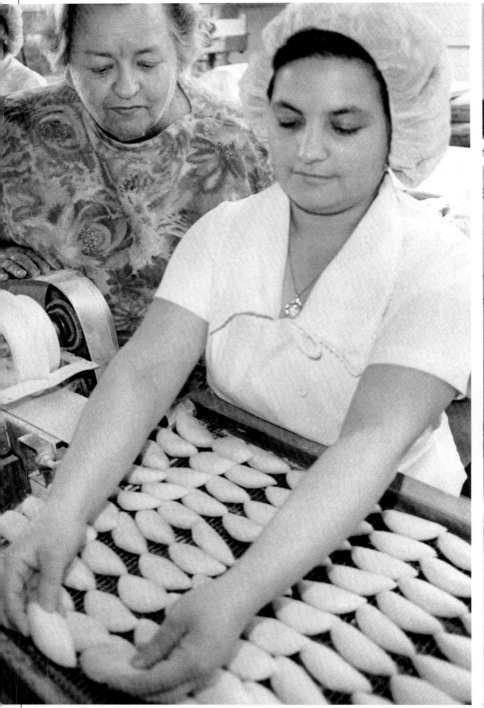

(Left) Preparing perogies at Naleway's (Mrs. Ann Naleway in background) (1974)

(Right) Junior's President John Philopulos with Anna Tsakiris and George Philopulos behind the counter (1979)

38-6484-65

Fred Jewell photo 38-6485-70

(Above) McGregor
(April, 1956)

(Below) Emerson
(April, 1965)

☐ **FLOODED TOWNS**

Morris (April, 1978)

FASHION Sportswear LTD.

Safe

Gregg Burner photo 39-3063-22

(Clockwise) Souris (April, 1976);
Ste. Anne (June, 1959); Rosenort (1979)

Frank Chalmers photo 39-3063-115

TOURIST CAMP
—CABINS—
SWIMMING BOATING
STE ANNE

38-6487-86

☐ FLOODING IN WINNIPEG

(Above) A Metro Transit bus didn't make it through the flooded McPhillips Street subway (August, 1966).

(Opposite) Steve Fortin of 2 Camrose Bay sitting in his new recreation room (July, 1968)

☐ ☐ ☐ ☐ ☐

City Flood at Crisis; Army in Control

THE WINNIPEG TRIBUNE

FINAL EDITION

ALL CITY DIKES BROKEN

Tribune Flood Edition Sunday

Hundreds Flee Suburb Homes

Morton Directs Aid Plan

Victims Flee New Red Tide

Trapped Worker Drowns

Evacuation Race Clears Hospitals

City Jail Moves Prisoners As Floods Cut Heat in Cells

Tribune Carrier Boys Fight Through City Flood

Residents of Kingston Row returned to their homes and spread their belongings outside to dry after flood waters receded in 1950.

Randy Fedeluk (front, age 12) and Fred Sutton (rear, age 14) canoing down
Melrose Avenue (July, 1968)

Jon Thordarson photo 37-2314-14

☐ THE FORT GARRY COURT FIRE

BEHIND THE CAMERA

JON THORDARSON: "This was a bitter cold day, the day after the Fort Garry Court fire. They wouldn't let her in to her apartment. It was an interesting follow-up because I was at the fire and saw all the chaos and the fatalities, and here's one lady who survived. Pat Flynn was the reporter. We made sure that she put the list away and was shuffled off before the *Free Press* or anyone else came along."

☐ ☐ ☐ ☐ ☐

(Above) Firemen rescue a victim.

(Opposite) Photographer's note (February 2, 1976): "Anne-Marie Laudi with long list of possessions left in bldg.

37-2314-10

(Above) A tragic blaze in the Fort Garry Court on February 1, 1976 killed 5 people and left 175 homeless.

(Left) The Fort Garry Court Building (shown in 1962 from the front of the CN Railway Depot) was a stately structure at the northwest corner of Main and Broadway with retail outlets at the street level and apartments on the upper floors.

65-5627-16

☐ GAMES OF CHESS

(Above) Central Park in 1962

(Right) Winnipeg chess expert Abe Yanofsky played the USSR's Boris Spaaski in 1967. Yanofsky was a chess prodigy as a child and became Canada's first Grand Master

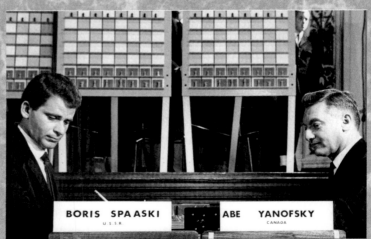

71-6247-5

BORIS SPAASKI U.S.S.R. **ABE YANOFSKY** CANADA

28-1530-5

Jim Walker photo 44-2770-9

(Left) Protest at the CBC
(1977)

(Below) Gay Liberation
Parade (1974)

(Opposite) Gay rights
advocates Chris Vogel and
Richard North (1974)

Jim Walker photo 44-2770-7

GAY RIGHTS IN THE '70S

PICTURING MANITOBA **Legacies of the Winnipeg Tribune**

Jeff De Booy photo 44-2770-21

18-780-10

18-780-13

1957; (Inset) The Prince Edward Hotel (1955)

GLIMPSES OF BRANDON

Jeff De Booy photo 18-780-48

Aerial view (1973)

Jeff De Booy photo 18-780-43

Frank Chalmers photo 33-1899-83

☐ GO GO DANCERS

Joe McLellan photo 33-1899-82

☐ ☐ ☐ ☐ ☐

(Above) An exotic dancer did her "bathtub act" for beverage room patrons (1973).

(Left) "The Dancing Swede" performed for noon-hour restaurant customers (1980).

44-2717-34

(Top) The Hecla Island
Ferry; (Below) The Village
of Hecla

44-2717-36

HECLA ISLAND, 1953

10120-11

THE HEATED AUTOPAC DEBATE

THE HEATED AUTOPAC DEBATE

50A-3681-31

(Above) Manitoba Government Employees Association President Gary Doer insisted that a 1979 review (published when the Sterling Lyon Conservatives were in power) "ignores Autopac's strengths."

(Top Right) Insurance agents envisioned the loss of their jobs and businesses as they picketed in April, 1970. Public automobile insurance was implemented in November, 1971.

(Right) Cars filled the streets of Wawanesa in 1969 as protestors rallied against public auto insurance, a plank in the platform of the Schreyer New Democrats when they formed Manitoba's first NDP government that year. Critics denounced the concept as a socialist scheme.

50A-3681-18

160

PICTURING MANITOBA **Legacies of the Winnipeg Tribune**

Frank Chalmers photo 50A-3681-17

Insurance agents and their supporters rallied at the Legislature in 1970 to oppose the pending legislation.

IN WINNIPEG AT CHRISTMAS

(Top & Far Left) Two Jim Wiley photos told the story of Winnipeg's official Christmas tree in 1977. The 35-foot (10.6 metre) blue spruce donated by Mr. and Mrs. J. Hawkins of 341 Queenston Street was loaded on as flatbed truck and lowered into position in the City Hall courtyard.

(Left) Santa and his reindeer in the 1976 Santa Claus Parade

29-1584-35

Gregg Burner photo 29-1584-84

The wise men were put in place in 1974 on the Great-West Life Building on Osborne. This was the second year for the display.

Jon Thordarson photo 69-7007-166

☐ KIDS BEING KIDS

☐ ☐ ☐ ☐ ☐

Published caption (August 8, 1980): "Five Transcona youngsters silhouetted in a puddle on the roof of Central school made instruments from scraps in a parks and recreation summer program"

E WIRE STORY —AM—Marbles (Budget)
NNIPEG OUT (wpg 2) Winnipeg, June 16—TENSE MOMENT—Aaron Cormie, 11, takes
eady to shoot while fellow marble players of John M. King School in Winnipeg
nnies has seen a resurgence in marble playing. (CP Laserphoto) 1980 (Winnip

(Top) Photographer's note (November 8, 1969): "A patrol has to put up with a lot (Debbie Dunlop, Bruce McLay, James McIsaac)."

(Left) Jeff De Booy went along for the ride.

BEHIND THE CAMERA

JEFF DE BOOY: "It was a summer evening and I was working nights when I saw this group of kids. I shot it at a slow shutter speed so I could get the background blurry. I sat on the merry-go-round."

Jeff De Booy photo

Jeff De Booy photo 28-1540-19

Precious Blood students found this slick sidewalk on Kenny Street made a great slide

BEHIND THE CAMERA

JEFF DE BOOY: "It happened to be a morning when it was cold and it had rained and iced over. I was actually looking for vehicles that were sliding down the slope off St. Mary's and it just happened these kids were going to school. .They really hammed it up for the camera."

Frank Chalmers photo 69-6069-138

Frank Chalmers photo 69-6069-123

THE LEGENDARY
MARCH 4th BLIZZARD

(Above) Snowdrifts reached the eaves and blocked the doors of home across southern Manitoba, including these Garden City bungalows.

(Above, Right) Vehicles on Wellington Avenue in Winnipeg's west end were going nowhere on March 4, 1966. A 21-hour blizzard paralyzed southern Manitoba with over 14 inches (36 cm) of snow blown into daunting drifts by 50 mile-per-hour (80 km) winds

69-6069-140

The blizzard forced Winnipeggers to spend the night wherever they happened to be. The bedding department in the Simpson Sears Polo Park store became a temporary dormitory for stranded women customers and staff, while men bedded down in the main floor shoe department on sleeping bags borrowed from the sporting goods department.

69-6069-137

33-2528-4

(Above) Boarding the school bus (1954); (Left) A Mountie writing a ticket (1954)

☐ LIFE IN DAUPHIN

33-2528-15

Frank Chalmers photo 66-5711-15

36-2258-232

Plumas ladies were ready with the lunch for a "feed-in"
during a 1968 "seed-in" at Gladstone and Plumas.

(Top) Harvesting in 1952

(Bottom) Potato grading near Winkler in 1956

CASANOVAS
BIG NIGHT

COFFEE SHOP

Selkirk (ca 1954)

62-5170-16

68-6003-8

☐ MAIN STREET, MANITOBA

(Above) Virden (1959); (Right) MacGregor (1964)

49-4231-4

47-3184-1

(Above) Killarney (1957)
(Below) Minnedosa (1956)

Hugh Allan photo 52-3899-10

63-5327-2

(Above) Souris (ca 1953);
(Left) Baldur (1965)

72-6475-83

The Main Street strip (1959)

MAIN STREET, WINNIPEG

45-2794-36

72-6475-35

72-6261-150

(Clockwise) Main and Higgins (1953);
Main Street south of St. Mary (1961);
Main Street south of Bannatyne
(1963)

MANITOBA ARTIFACTS

Jon Thordarson photo 50-4267-9

Bruno Rivard photo 50-4267-12

Joe McLellan photo 50-4267-11

Jon Thordarson photo 50-4267-8

Jim Walker photo 50-4322-4337-95

MANITOBA'S LEGISLATURE

The House in session (1980)

(Right) Looking for a "weather shot," Jeff De Booy spotted a man walking down Broadway past the Legislature and asked if he could take his picture. (December, 1975)

Jeff De Booy photo 68-6069A-96

A view of the main staircase (1975)

Jon Thordarson photo 42-2601-10

☐ MANITOBA'S LIQUOR LAWS

Near Broadway and Osborne in 1979

☐ ☐ ☐ ☐ ☐

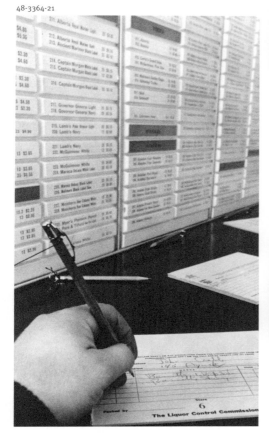

48-3364-21

25-647-12

(Clockwise)
Customers in government liquor
stores in 1967 were required to write
their orders on forms and take them
to a clerk at the counter

Beer waitresses in 1958

Government liquor stores in 1957
displayed single bottles of the
products available. Male clerks filled
customers' orders from a storage
room in the back of the store.

48-3364-20

42-2518-6

MAYORS AND THEIR TOWNS

Jon Thordarson photo 10135-2

(Above) Mayor John Paxton of Gladstone (1957)

(Left) Published caption (April 28, 1979): "Emerson mayor Ralph Eisbrenner stands on dike holding back the swollen Red River from his town's Main Street 10 feet below

(Clockwise)
Mayor E. O. Walterson of Beausejour (1974)

Mayor Dick Penner of Altona (1976)

Published caption (June 19, 1980): St. Lazare Mayor Omer Chartier, who says he'll believe a potash boom in his area when he sees it, chats with Josephine Deschambault

Mayor Ken Mikolayenko on the main street of Ethelbert (1975)

10655-10

Frank Chalmers photo 10375-4

61-5061-2

Jeff De Booy photo 10431-12

MEMORABLE WINNIPEG FIRES

37-2314-52

Hans Deryk photo 37-2315-89

(Above) The Furby Theatre, 597 Portage Avenue (February, 1952); (Right) Holiday Inn, St. Mary Avenue (July, 1980); (Opposite) St. Andrews United Church, 415 Elgin Avenue (November, 1968)

37-2314-46

Ernie Einarsson photo 37-2314-54

(Clockwise)
The Kresge Building, 368 Portage
Avenue (March, 1973)

Minto Armouries, St. Matthews
Avenue at Minto Street (January,
1956

Wilson Furniture, 279-281 Rupert
Avenue (February, 1958)

37-2307-41

22-344-7

☐ THE MILITARY IN MANITOBA

22-342-1

(Above) The Canadian Women's Army Corps (1941)

(Left) The Winnipeg Grenadiers marching south on Main Street (1941)

☐ ☐ ☐ ☐ ☐

22-342-9

(Top) The Winnipeg Grenadiers departing for Hong Kong (ca 1941)

(Right) Marching in the rain – a Royal Canadian Legion parade in 1976

BEHIND THE CAMERA

GREGG BURNER: "We were all trying to copy somebody, feeling our way through photography, so you look at the masters. Henri Cartier-Bresson was the godfather of the candid picture. There was a transformation taking place between a set-up picture - which you had to do in the really old days because the cameras weren't that sophisticated, so you posed everybody – as opposed to the candid."

Gregg Burner photo 27-1341-3

36-2244-4

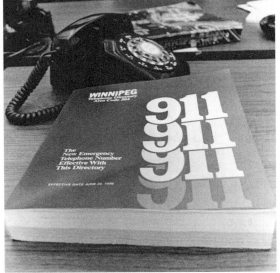

50A-3704-2

☐ ON THE PHONE

(Above) A Family Bureau office in 1957

(Left) In 1959, Winnipeg became the first city in North America to implement an emergency phone number system, with 999 able to reach emergency services. At the time, the Winnipeg area had 16 municipalities, each with its own police department and fire department, resulting in a 32 different phone numbers. The 999 number was later changed to 911 to achieve uniformity across the continent.

(Opposite) This award-winning 1979 Jim Wiley photo showed a Portage Avenue pedestrian who was determined to make a phone call.

☐ ☐ ☐ ☐ ☐

TELEPHONE

6P1
MANITOBA

34-2018-3

Jeff De Booy photo 72-6261-171

(Above) Photographer's note (1976): "Was cruisin' strictly a '50's phenomenon or are today's youth still driving the streets and filling the parking lots of drive-ins?

(Right) Taxidermist Ken Hawkins found an unusual way to make a delivery in 1969.

24-639-24

10116-5

Empire Hotel
The FINEST IN FOOD

John Diefenbaker (left) and Duff
Roblin strolled north on Winnipeg's
Main Street away from the CNR
depot (1959).

☐ PERSONALITIES IN POLITICS

Jim Walker photo 10082-2

Jeff De Booy photo 10044-12

Published caption (May 9, 1979): "While visiting
Morris, Joe Clark talks with troops manning dikes"

(Right) Published caption (May 28, 1980): "Manitoba
NDP Leader Howard Pawley (right) listens as federal
leader Ed Broadbent fields questions"

☐ ☐ ☐ ☐ ☐

(Left) This shot of John Diefenbaker in a typical stance as he opened the 1962 federal campaign before an overflow crowd at the Winnipeg Auditorium was one of Gordon Aikman's favourites.

(Below) Trib editor Bud Sherman went on to a successful career in politics. Here he is with his wife Liz-Ann in May, 1968.

(Bottom) Hugh Allan captured this shot of Duff Roblin and his bagpipes in 1952.

10556-15

Gordon Aikman photo courtesy of Katie Chalmers-Brooks

Hugh Allan photo 10482-2

Gregg Burner photo 10142-13

(Above) Gregg Burner's camera revealed how the diminutive Tommy Douglas (Douglas was about 5'5") compensated for a tall podium while speaking in Winnipeg in 1970.

(Right) Prime Minister Lester Pearson and his wife Maryon chatted with some Hutterite women in Winkler in 1965.

10429-2

Lord Roberts Community Club (1970)

30-1178-47

☐ PLAYING AT THE COMMUNITY CLUBS

Hunter photo 30-1178-96

30-1178-73

30-1178-75

(Clockwise) Chalmers Community
Club (1967); Norquay Community Club
(1967); North Kildonan Community
Club (1967)

☐ ☐ ☐ ☐ ☐

The telegram reads:

DR. JONAS E. SALK, DIRECTOR OF VIRUS RESEARCH LAB, SCHOOL OF MEDICINE, UNIVERSITY OF PENNSYLVANIA, PITTSBURGH, PENNSYLVANIA, U.S.A.

INSPIRING DISCOVERY OF SALK POLIO VACCINE WILL MEAN MUCH TO WHOLE WORLD AND ESPECIALLY THE PEOPLE OF MANITOBA WHOSE LIVES WERE RAVAGED BY DEVASTATING 1953 EPIDEMIC.

THEREFORE WE SEND OUR HEARTFELT APPRECIATION OF YOUR DEDICATED PATIENCE GIVING US NEW HOPE THAT OUR CHILDREN MAY GROW UNHAMPERED BY CRIPPLING AFFLICTION. FREEDOM FROM FEAR OF FUTURE POLIO RAVAGES CHEERS AND HEARTENS OUR FAMILIES.

WILL YOU AND YOUR ASSOCIATES IN THIS HISTORY MAKING ACCOMPLISHMENT ACCEPT THE DEEP GRATITUDE OF THE PEOPLE OF MANITOBA.

BROADCASTING STATION CKY
THESE...

A telegram with the names of over 8,000 Manitobans thanking Dr. Jonas Salk, for developing the vaccine that virtually eliminated polio was sent by radio station CKY in April, 1955. It was 200 feet (60 metres) long and took eight hours to send.

POLIO

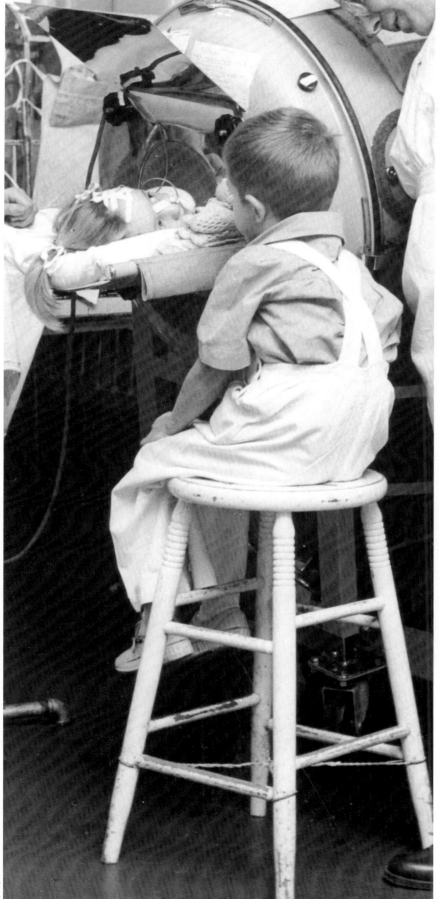

56-4561-18

56-4561-47

(Clockwise) "Iron lungs" (mechanical respirators to help patients breathe) were shipped from across North America for use in Manitoba in the early 1950s. Most polio patients were children. (1952 photo)

Although earlier years had seen smaller outbreaks of poliomyelitis in Manitoba, there were more than 2,500 cases of the paralyzing disease in the province in 1953

Projecting a movie on the ceiling for a patient in an iron lung (1956)

56-4561-58

☐ POLITICIANS AND THEIR FAMILIES

☐ ☐ ☐ ☐ ☐

(Above) Gary Filmon with his son David, daughter Allison, and wife Janice on his re-election to City Council in October, 1977

(Right) Bill Norrie with his son Mark after his election as Mayor of Winnipeg in 1977. Norrie remained mayor until 1992

Pearl McGonigal and family (1979). McGonigal was a member of Winnipeg
City Council from 1971 to 1981 and was Manitoba's first woman Lieutenant
Governor from 1981 to 1986.

□ □ □ □ □

(Below) Pierre Trudeau and his sons Justin, Michael, and Sasha in Winnipeg (1977)

(Right) Israel Asper and son David campaigning in the 1973 provincial election. Izzy Asper became the Leader of the Manitoba Liberal Party in 1970, won a seat in the 1973 election, and resigned from active politics in 1975

Frank Chalmers photo 10629-13

Gerry Hart photo 10013-3

10485-5

(Above) Duff Roblin with son Stephen Andrew (1962)

(Left) The Schreyer family in 1965: Karmel (1 1/2), Lily, Lisa (3 1/2), Ed

10524-4

63-5230-19

22-344-7

56-5389-3

56-5389-1

☐ POLO PARK: FROM HORSE RACES TO SHOPPING

(Clockwise)
A view of the shopping centre from the parking lot (1960)

Polo Park Race Track in the early 1950s

Polo Park Shopping Centre was an outdoor mall in 1959.

☐ ☐ ☐ ☐ ☐

Ron Dobson photo 25-687-14

25-687-9

☐ **POOL HALLS**

☐ ☐ ☐ ☐ ☐

(Above, Left) Concentrating on the game at the Orpheum (1979)

(Right) Eddie Tysowski (left) and Phil Heiland (right) in the Orpheum Pool Hall (1980)

25687-6

(Above) The Orpheum Pool Hall on Fort Street (1980)

(Left) Ed Koranicki at Eddy's Place (1979)

25-687-13

CHILDS BUILDING

CANADIAN NATIONAL RAILWAYS
TRANS-CANADA AIR LINES

LOANS
HOUSEHOLD FINANCE
HFC

72-6475-36

Gerry Hart photo 66-5672-11

(Above) The southwest corner in 1973;

(Below) The northwest corner in 1974

Jeff De Booy photo 70-6191-23

35-2145-11

36-2236-9

☐ THE PROSPECT OF NUCLEAR WAR

(Above) An artist's
impression of the impact
of a nuclear bomb on
downtown Winnipeg (1953)

(Left) The comforts of home
in a fallout shelter (1960)

33-1969-49

"9 MILE MARCH" FROM EDGE OF TOTAL DESTRUCTION ONE H-BOMB AT PORTAGE + MAIN

WINNIPEG COMMITTEE FOR DISARMAMENT

NUCLEAR ARMS CANA...

23-464-1

PRESIDENT KENNEDY ....

"STOP THE TESTS"

TOO MUCH STRONTIU... ALREAD...

12 HOUR VIGIL AGAINST NUCLEAR TESTING

NIPEG TRIBUNE

Weekend MAGAZINE

...RDAY, JANUARY 26, 1963   10 CENTS   ★★ PHONE WHitehall 2-8101

...ion may be taken in May

M straddles nuclear fence;
...ves NATO role in doubt

We will fulfill pact: Harkness

By Charles Lynch
Southam News Service

OTTAWA — Canada undertook in 1959 to play a nuclear role in NATO, but that role has now been placed under doubt and may have to be re-negotiated, Prime Minister Diefenbaker told the House of Commons Friday.

The prime minister's statement left the way open for the government to fulfill the nuclear undertaking, or to veer away from it into a conventional role and abandon half a billion dollars worth of nuclear carriers, notably the CF-104 Starfighter jets.

Outside the House, Defence Minister Harkness said the prime minister's statement meant the nuclear undertaking would be fulfilled.

Mr. Diefenbaker seemed to confirm this by announcing that negotiations were proceeding with the United States on a bi-lateral agreement under which nuclear warheads could be made available to Canadian forces, both home defence and NATO, under joint control and ...

WARMER, BUT NOT SOON . . .

Winnipeg shivered through its 10th consecutive day of below zero weather today but the weatherman indicated relief is in sight.

A mass of milder air moved through Alaska Friday and is ...

23-470-1

Protect your family wit... BASEMENT FALLOUT SHELTER

WINNIPEG SUPPLY

36-2236-6

(Clockwise)
Nuclear arms protestors (1962)

"Ban the Bomb" marchers outside The Tribune Building (1962)

Provincial cabinet minister Gurney Evans inspecting a fallout shelter (1960)

PRESENT
JACKPOT

RATE OF
GROWTH

AMPEX

George McCloy, CJOB (1964)

10329-9

Jim Walker photo 27-905-4

☐ **RADIO DAYS** (Clockwise) Lorraine, "The First Lady of Radio," CKY (1978); Red Alix, CJOB (1966); Donn Kirton, CKY and CJOB (1979) ☐ ☐ ☐ ☐ ☐

Jeff De Booy photo   22-344-7

(Left) Terry Klassen, CITI-FM ;
(Above) Bob Irving, CJOB (1980)

10658-12

22-344-7

(Above) Bob Washington, CKRC (1979);
(Left) Cliff Gardner, CJOB and CKRC
(1974)

60-5030-58

Frank Chalmers photo 60-5030-7

Frank Chalmers photo 59-4915-69

☐ REVISITING ST. BONIFACE

(Clockwise) A 1976 view of Provencher Boulevard; Precious Blood Church, 1968; City of St. Boniface Mayoralty candidates in 1968 (left to right) Don Hart, Georges Forest, George Provost, Edward Turner

Gregg Burner photo 33-1868-15

10686-2

LAUNDERERS CLEANERS FURRIERS

EAST

33-1868-7

(Clockwise) Jam Pail Curling (1975); The Olympic Rink (1962); Curling greats Howard Wood (left) and Billy Walsh chatting over a cup of coffee (1957)

☐ THE ROARING GAME

☐ ☐ ☐ ☐ ☐

☐ ROCK CONCERTS

John Olson photo 59-4902-9

Rock festival at the Ponderosa (July, 1970)

☐ ☐ ☐ ☐ ☐

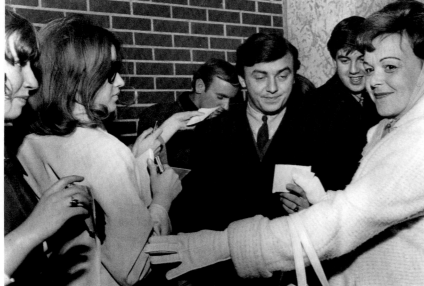

10180-9

(Clockwise) Monkees fan at the
arena (1967); A Herman's Hermits
fan got carried away (1967); Getting
an autograph from Gerry Marsden
of Gerry and the Pacemakers at the
airport (1965)

10502-9

Restraining some Monkees
fans (1967)

33-1843-11

THE ROYAL ALEX

(Right) The Royal Alexandra Hotel (shown here in 1963) opened in 1906, a grand hotel of the Canadian Pacific Railway. Known affectionately to Winnipeggers as "The Royal Alex," the palatial structure at the corner of Higgins and Main ranked, along with its Canadian National Railways counterpart the Fort Garry, as the finest in the city for luxurious accommodations, fine cuisine, and grand occasions

(Below Right) In July 1971, the Royal Alexandra Hotel was being dismantled

(Below Left) The Selkirk Room;.

28-1375-11

28-1375-7

28-1375-23

28-1375-1

28-1375-14

(Above) By the early 1970s, the sunshine of rail travel had been eclipsed by air travel, the Main Street area had deteriorated, and the Royal Alex had lost its splendour. A lone security guard made his rounds in March of 1971 through the once-glamourous Alexandra Room as the hotel was prepared for demolition

(Left) The Vice-Regal Suite

☐ ROYALTY COMES TO CALL

(Left) Portage la Prairie, 1970;
(Below) Clear Lake, 1970

Frank Chalmers photo 60-4980-66

Hugh Allan photo 60-4980-12

10068-3

John Olson photo 46-3619-2

Frank Chalmers photo 34-1984-72

Max the daschund inspected the lines during a fire drill at St. John's-Ravenscourt School in 1970.

Frank Chalmers photo 34-2078-66

(Left) Students at Robert Smith School in Selkirk and principal Tony Maksymyk viewed a solar eclipse in March, 1979

(Below) Breaking a trail at St. John's Cathedral Boys School in 1969

61-5052-14

45-2814-8

45-2814-13

45-2814-33

☐ ☐ ☐ ☐ ☐

Firemen battled the blaze
with little success

59-4922-16

THE ST. BONIFACE CATHEDRAL FIRE

(Clockwise)
Stunned parishoners stared silently at the shell of their church

On July 22, 1968, the St. Boniface Cathedral (consecrated in 1908) was gutted by fire, leaving only the façade and outer walls

Archbishop Maurice Badoux watched as flames decimated the cathedral

Archbishop Baudoux stood outside the ravaged church with some salvaged furniture.

59-4922-32

Hugh Allan photo 59-4922-13

59-4922-25

59-4922-4

Joe McLellen photo 28-1364-49

(Above) Published caption (October 1, 1979): "At one time hundreds of people filled the station's waiting room (CN station). Now, benches sit almost empty even during the busy periods"

(Left) The CPR yards from Salter Bridge looking west (1962)

28-1381-58

☐ THE TWO RAILWAYS

The CN depot was commemorated as an historic site by Parks Canada in 1978.

28-1381-69

Jeff De Booy photo 28-1381-64

28-1381-44

(Clockwise)
The CP Rail station in 1964; Interior of the CP Rail station (1978); CP Rail utilized special 15-auto railway cars for shipping vehicles (1962).

The CN Depot (Union Station) at Main and Broadway (1978)

Art Carter photo 65-5605-88

☐ TORNADOES OF SUMMER

(Above) Published caption (June 21, 1978): "Three South Carolina journalists were traveling in the Aubigny area Monday when they photographed this funnel cloud at about 5:30 pm."

(Right) La Riviere (July, 1968)

☐ ☐ ☐ ☐ ☐

65-5605-92

65-5605-67

(Top) A school bus was blown about 50 yards (46 metres) and came to rest on a Volkswagen. Aubigny (June, 1978

(Right) The Pas (July, 1979)

65-5605-59

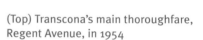

(Top) Transcona's main thoroughfare, Regent Avenue, in 1954

(Left) Transcona was established in the early 1900s when the Grand Trunk Pacific Railway purchased 800 acres (3.24 square kilometres) of land 8 miles (12.8 kilometres) east of Winnipeg for railway repair shops and a town site. The CNR Transcona Shops (shown here at a shift change in 1954) were the lifeblood of the community for decades

TRANSCONA IN THE '50s

66-6524-6525-9

(Left) Mayor J. S. Johnson was himself a railway man (1954 photo).

(Below) A 1955 billboard welcomed visitors to Transcona.

66-6524-6525-10

SAM the CAMERAMAN
UNDERSELLS EVERYONE

VOLKSWAGEN

ST. MARY

COLONY

THE MALL

Excavation for the Winnipeg Art Gallery,
photographed from the roof of the Hudson's
Bay store (January, 1970)

WINNIPEG LANDMARKS IN PROGRESS

Jim Walker photo 64-5477-11

(Clockwise)
Repainting the lines in the Pan Am Pool in 1978. Draining the 800,000 gallon (3.6 million litre) pool took 20 hours.

Future site of The Forks (1972)

Moving the Nonsuch to the Museum of Man and Nature (November, 1973)

Tec-Voc High School under construction (February, 1950)

53-4198-33

Gerry Hart photo 70-6188-10

65-5523-1

Frank Chalmers photo 66-5672-31

Jim Worobec photo 51-4510-28

(Clockwise)
Excavating for the Trizec Building, photographed from the roof of the Richardson Building (June, 1977)

The Manitoba Theatre Centre under construction (October, 1969)

Construction of the underground concourse at Portage and Main (December, 1977)

Jon Thordarson photo 72-6272-24

PICTURING MANITOBA **Legacies of the Winnipeg Tribune**

Gerry Hart photo 30-1214-22

(Above) Two workers on the catwalk of a crane during the construction of the Woodsworth Building in 1973. Photographer Gerry Hart, despite his fear of heights, was on the crane with them. The partly-completed Winnipeg Convention Centre can be seen in the background

(Right) Excavating for the Richardson Building (March, 1967)

Hugh Allan photo 72-6261-94

70-7120-3

WINNIPEG'S CITY HALLS

Hugh Allan photo 70-7120-7

70-7120-51

(Above) Princess St looking east to Main St and the rear of the City Hall in 1957, with a market garden in the foreground

(Far Left) Winnipeg new Civic Centre under construction in April, 1964

(Left) The Council Chamber in the old City Hall (1957)

Few buildings in Winnipeg's history have provoked as wide a range of emotions as its Victorian-style City Hall. With its bizarre adornment of turrets and ornamental brick and stone, the design exemplified the optimism Winnipeggers shared for the future of their thriving little city (population 20,238) when the building opened in 1886. Decades later, the distinctive structure, nicknamed the "Gingerbread City Hall", was loved by some and reviled by others. In 1962, with its tower crumbling and its plaster falling, the beloved and abused icon was demolished to make way for a modern new Civic Centre.

☐ **WINNIPEG'S GOLDEN AGE OF ROCK**

☐ ☐ ☐ ☐ ☐ (Above) Crowcuss in 1977: (left to right) Hermann Fruhm, Greg Leskiw, Larry Pink, Marc La France, Bill Wallace

(Right) A 1971 file photo of Sugar'n'Spice: (left to right) Reid O'Connell, Glen Stewart, Laurie Currie, Aileen Murphy, Brian Meissner, Chuck Gorling

Sugar 'n' Spice

Booked Exclusively By
HUNGRY i AGENCY

Jim Wiley photo 10206-5

10384-8

(Clockwise)
Harlequin in 1976: (left to right)
David Budzak, Ralph James, Gary
Golden, Leroy Hawk, George
Belanger

The Mongrels in 1967: (left to right)
John Nykon, Larry Rassmuson, Garth
Noseworthy, Duncan Wilson, Joey
Gregorash

A 1971 photo of The Guess Who

☐ ☐ ☐ ☐ ☐

10197-1

☐ WINNIPEG'S NEW CENTENNIAL CENTRE

(Above) Future site of the concert hall, museum, and planetarium in 1964

(Right) The arts centre under construction in March, 1967

Fred Jewell photo 28-1486-86

WINNIPEG'S BUSY AIRPORT

(Clockwise)
Buying some insurance before the flight (1959)

Named Stevenson Field in 1928 to honour pioneer bush pilot Frederick Stevenson, the facility was renamed Winnipeg International Airport in 1958. The aging terminal was replaced in 1964

The official opening of the new Winnipeg International Airport terminal in 1964

73-6332-4

Hugh Allan photo 73-6332-26

73-6332-102

☐ WINNIPEG'S POLICE DEPARTMENTS

34-2719-16

65-5627-97

76-6473-16

(Clockwise)
Chief Chris Einfeld, City of East
Kildonan Police Department, and his
men (1968)

Explaining the rules to pedestrians
(1966)

Using a police call box (1951)

71-6254-175

The "Bobby" helmets worn by Winnipeg Police until the early 1950s didn't fit modern cars.

10327-16

(Above) Chief Donald MacDonald, City of St. James Police Department (1956)

Jeff De Booy photo 68-6055-7

(Above) Plans to build underground public washrooms with a bunker-like entrance in Memorial Park in 1973 became a major political issue that was dubbed the Great Biffy Debate

(Right) Mayor Stephen Juba clashed with pro-biffy advocates and Public Works Minister Russell Doern (1973)

Jim Walker photo 68-6055-5

☐ WINNIPEG'S PUBLIC RESTROOMS

68-6055-4

(Above) The Logan Avenue Comfort Station (south side of Logan just east of Main), 1967

(Right) The city's last downtown public comfort station at Portage and Garry closed in 1978. The washroom facilities were located underground.

Jim Walker photo 68-6055-6

Jon Thordarson photo 10209-1

10510-8

22-344-7

(Clockwise)
John Harvard, CBWT (1977); Sylvia Kuzyk,
CJAY/CKY-TV (1977); Ed Russenholt,
CBWT (1954) Ray Torgrud, CJAY/CKY-TV
(1966)

(Clockwise)
"Reach for the Top" personalities Bill Guest (left) and Lionel Moore with makeup artist Cecille Lanthier, CBWT (1973)

Adrienne Clarkson and Peter Herrndorf, CBC (1976)

"Manitoba" Tonight on CKND-TV (1979) (clockwise from bottom right) Marjorie Salki, Brian Swain, Andy Arnot, Kevin Evans

65-5546-30

☐ WINNIPEG'S TELEVISION STATIONS

27-903-1

10217-8

Gregg Burner photo 67-5936-51

Exam time at the U of M (April, 1971)

Frank Chalmers photo 67-5938-33

(Above) The University of Winnipeg received its charter in 1967, establishing it as a degree-granting institution

(Right) Waiting for the bus at the University of Manitoba in the 1950s

40-2386-34

74-5660-14

74-5660-9

74-5660-8

In September, 1957, a group of neighbourhood women linked arms to
prevent a City of Winnipeg crew from cutting down a huge century-old triple-
trunked elm tree that stood in the middle of Wolseley Avenue. With its own
curb and tiny patch of grass, the tree had been described by Ripley's Believe
It or Not as the smallest park in the world.

With police and reporters present, the determined women defended the life
of the Wolseley Elm. Local residents, particularly mothers of young children,
appreciated its ability to slow down traffic on Wolseley. City officials saw
the tree as a safety hazard for motorists, especially football fans who used
Wolseley as a shortcut to Bomber games at the Arena.

Recently-elected mayor Steve Juba, ever the folk hero (especially when
reporters were nearby) came to the rescue in his Cadillac. He sent the
demolition crew away and earned the applause of the protesters.

Although Juba and the neighbourhood women earned the elm a reprieve, it
was attacked on three occasions in 1958: first by arsonists, then by vandals
with crowbars and saws, and finally with (on Halloweeen) with dynamite.
Tree surgeon Alex Gudziak tried to save the legendary tree without success.

Finally, in July, 1960, the famed Wolseley Elm was pronounced dead and was
removed.

The Winnipeg Tribune

The Final Edition

Wednesday, August 27, 1980

No. 201

been 90 great years!

message ... publisher

Readers and advertisers responded and today's circulation is more than 50 per cent greater than in 1975. The share of the advertising market has also increased each year until it is now approaching 45 per cent. Unfortunately, increasing revenues have not kept up with inflating costs and each year the costs have been greater.

I am sure that in time The Tribune would have become the largest circulation newspaper in

See MESSAGE, Page 5

made this ... by its

note to you. It is sadder in every way

... er in Canada. ... 5 it has been ... an innovator ... mic book and

Tribune ceases publication

Southam Inc. president Gordon Fisher informs Tribune employees that the paper will cease publication after 90 years.

The Winnipeg Tribune ceases publication with this edition.

The announcement was made to Tribune employees at 9 a.m. today by Gordon Fisher, president of Southam Inc.

Mr. Fisher said that in the past five years since the New Trib was launched, total losses have exceeded $16 million, including the $3 million anticipated loss for 1980.

"It is with the deepest regret and after the most careful analysis that Southam's board of directors has reached this painful decision," Mr. Fisher said.

E.H. Wheatley, publisher of the Tribune, spoke of his own sorrow and unhappiness caused by the closure of The Trib.

"The Trib team has been a great one to work with and I am deeply and sincerely saddened at the closure of the paper," he said. "However, I do accept its inevitability."

Southam has owned The Tribune since 1920. The Tribune, now in its 90th year, fell into a loss position in 1969 and has been unable to capture the dominant position over its competitor, The Winnipeg Free Press.

In 1975, in an attempt to recapture more of the market, Southam launched the New Trib in an aggressive recovery program that involved resources commitment of Southam corporate "resources without any certainty of eventual recovery," Mr. Fisher told the staff.

In the past five years, The Trib went from a circulation of 70,000 to one of approximately 100,000.

The Trib was among the most innovative papers in the country, at the forefront of change in terms of newspaper research, design, content and promotion. In addition to free personal want ads and the appointment of a full-time ombudsman, the Trib initiated such features as Trib Magazine and the Looking Good fashion section, the Trib Comic Book, the Trib Auto and Trib and Trib Monday sports tab, the Monday special sections, and other special sections in circulation and Homes, and other special sections.

"The Tribune's growth in circulation and advertising volume has now created a situation where productive capacity is near its limit and the company will shortly be faced with a major capital investment for which there would be no foreseeable payback," Mr. Fisher explained.

"In the final analysis we have concluded that Winnipeg is a market that will not support two viable daily newspapers."

The Tribune announcement came on the heels of a statement by Thomson Newspapers publication this morning Ottawa Journal ceases publication today.

"The circumstances in Ottawa are a mirror image of those in Winnipeg," Mr. Fisher said, citing "major operating losses without hope of future turn-around" and "the inevitable death of one of that city's traditional newspapers."

Southam also has announced that it has

See AFTER, Page 5

To our readers, advertisers and carriers, thanks.

It's been a special relationship.

—Trib staff